To

Anne + M ——o—m

HEALING THE NATION

GOD'S HEART FOR A
(dis)UNITED KINGDOM

Very Best wishes

Mannie Jones

Also part of the trilogy:

One God, One Plan, One Family ...
LIVING THE MESSAGE

and

TURNING THE TIDE
God's Heart Surgery for the Christian Church

HEALING THE NATION

GOD'S HEART FOR A
(dis)UNITED KINGDOM

MAURICE JONES

Copyright © 2010 Maurice Jones

The moral right of the author has been asserted.

Apart from any fair dealing for the purposes of research or private study,
or criticism or review, as permitted under the Copyright, Designs and Patents
Act 1988, this publication may only be reproduced, stored or transmitted, in
any form or by any means, with the prior permission in writing of the
publishers, or in the case of reprographic reproduction in accordance with
the terms of licences issued by the Copyright Licensing Agency. Enquiries
concerning reproduction outside those terms should be sent to the publishers.

Matador
5 Weir Road
Kibworth Beauchamp
Leicester LE8 0LQ, UK
Tel: (+44) 116 279 2299
Fax: (+44) 116 279 2277
Email: books@troubador.co.uk
Web: www.troubador.co.uk/matador

ISBN 978-1848762-800

British Library Cataloguing in Publication Data.
A catalogue record for this book is available from the British Library.

Unless otherwise indicated, "Scripture taken from the HOLY BIBLE, NEW
INTERNATIONAL VERSION. Copyright © 1973, 1978, 1984 International Bible Society.
Used by permission of Zondervan Bible Publishers."

Also cited:
The Holy Bible, Living Bible Edition, Copyright Tyndale House Publishers 1971,
Kingsway Publications Ltd, 1994

Typeset in 11pt Bembo by Troubador Publishing Ltd, Leicester, UK

Matador is an imprint of Troubador Publishing Ltd

Printed in Great Britain by the MPG Books Group, Bodmin and King's Lynn

For my mother Maureen and late father George, who brought me into the world and through many personal sacrifices, offered my brother Russell and me a childhood full of fun, love and security. Also for my in-laws, Josie and Owen Martin, who have supported and encouraged me in many ways since my marriage to their beautiful daughter Angie, without whose unending patience, love, assistance and wisdom, I would not have been able to complete this trilogy.

CONTENTS

INTRODUCTION

The Empire's New Clothes

Once upon a time there was a small kingdom whose citizens were very fond of visiting other kingdoms.

Most of the citizens in the other kingdoms were happy to keep themselves to themselves, but the small kingdom wished for an empire and began to rule over them.

Although the small kingdom, which had now become a great kingdom, tried to be a wise and just ruler, the other kingdoms did not feel they were being treated wisely or justly and one by one left the empire. The great kingdom became a small kingdom once again.

Years passed. Then, one day, two men from a village called Westminster addressed the citizens.

"We can make you into a great kingdom once again," they said,

"And, what is more, the way we achieve it will be invisible to anyone who is either foolish or unfit for office."

The citizens of the small kingdom thought how wise they would look if they allowed the two men to make them into a great kingdom. Also, they would discover who, in the small kingdom, was foolish and unfit for office.

"You must do what you can at once," they told them and, from that day on, the two men governed the small kingdom and worked late each night.

In time, the most important citizens in the small kingdom

were sent to consider what had been accomplished and the two men described in great detail everything they had achieved.

The most important citizens paid close attention to what they were told, for, unable to believe their ears, they wanted to be able to report exactly to the citizens of the small kingdom.

When the citizens heard their report they said,

"We must show all the other kingdoms everything the two men have achieved. They will then be able to see we are a great kingdom once again."

And so it was agreed to hold an amazing exhibition in a huge, dazzling white glass building shaped like an elephant.

When the exhibition was complete the two men sent out an invitation to all the important citizens.

The important citizens could scarcely believe their eyes and were very concerned at what they saw. But not wanting to appear foolish or unfit for office, they said nothing.

At last the day came for the exhibition to be opened. As they entered the building, each citizen proudly lifted their head and said excitedly, "We are a great kingdom once more!

Now all the other kingdoms will be able to see what has been achieved and how we are all benefiting."

However, as they walked inside the huge white elephant, the citizens became quieter and quieter. The important citizens thought to themselves, the exhibition must be so stunning that no one can find the right words to describe it.

Suddenly, a small child's voice could be clearly heard to say, "But the building is completely empty."

"It really is empty," the citizens echoed, each feeling secretly foolish not to have spoken up earlier.

What could the citizens of the small kingdom do now? Never had they felt so embarrassed in front of all the other kingdoms.

Then one important citizen said, "We may be a small kingdom but there are many things we can do well. Let's enjoy being what we are and stop trying to be something we are not."

The citizens of the small kingdom, realising the wisdom of

MAURICE JONES

these words, began to cheer more loudly than they had ever cheered before.

And, from that day on, the citizens of the small kingdom didn't try any longer to be a great kingdom but instead simply enjoyed doing what they did best.

And, as the people of the small kingdom demonstrated wisdom and justice to one another and began to work together, so they became known by all the other kingdoms as the 'small kingdom with the BIG heart.'

(Adapted from The Emperor's New Clothes)

It is reassuring to know that not only is God interested in the major events of history, but also in human relationships and the routine experiences of everyday living. However, for everyone, the routine experiences of everyday living are often affected in one way or another by those who have been given the authority to govern. Therefore, although God is far above the political arena, as politics is about people and God is deeply interested in people and what affects their lives, so He is deeply interested in politics.

God, though, is not seeking to disregard men's ideas, but give them direction. For, it is not the understanding of the United Kingdom's problems that has hindered progress, as most are well known and the answers well rehearsed. It is achieving a unity of mind on what path to follow in order to overcome them that has eluded people.

This disunity of mind has left the United Kingdom adrift in a sea of unresolved and seemingly unresolvable difficulties. It is now time therefore to begin a process of change, healing and reconciliation.

To start, however, we need to ask two questions.

Firstly, how did we get where we are as a nation and secondly, how can we move forward?

CHAPTER ONE

The Party Is Over

Goodbye Great Britain,
Holed beneath the water line.
"We'll fix the leak in time, in time."
The Captain laughed, the band played on
The passengers watched,
and cried,
and swam.
"We'll fix the leak, or at least we'll try,"
The Captain sings, as the drowned float by.

The Road to Conflict

I have never experienced the reality of war. When I was a child, my father, who served with the Royal Navy during the Second World War, often told me of his wartime experiences.

How he signed up under-age. How he travelled the world. How he enjoyed the comradeship and sense of purpose.

My mother, who was evacuated from London to Lincolnshire, likewise told me of the pain and horror of the blitz and the ever-haunting trauma of living with death daily. In August 1945, the United Kingdom, along with many other nations, celebrated victory on the battlefield and began the slow, painful process of reconstructing the broken pieces of life. It was a new start. An opportunity to create a society that promoted harmony, peace and unity. By now that process should have been complete. It is apparent, however, that the United

Kingdom is still at war. This time, though, not with an invading army, but internally.

On the home front, peace has yet to be declared. The United Kingdom has become disunited. A disunity that has led to disconnection. A disconnection that has brought people into disharmony and conflict, one with the other. We hear what people are saying, but we don't have time to listen to them.

We want to be a part of the local community and enjoy a sense of belonging, but in order to meet the needs of the wider economy we have become economic migrants. We know we are complex human beings with thoughts and feelings, but we have allowed others to define us simply as 'consumers', with no thoughts or feelings, only credit ratings.

We know that money doesn't buy love and friendship, but our commitment to constantly raising the level of our lifestyles means that raising our income has become our first priority. We want to build caring, meaningful relationships with others, particularly within our families, but we are persuaded to live self-centred lives. We know that there is strength in unity, but we have allowed the fear and misunderstanding that segregation encourages to discourage us from real contact with our neighbours, those with whom we share this island and those with whom we share the world. The collective impact of these transient and distant relationships has been a breakdown in mutual understanding and trust, a draining away of social cohesion and respect.

Unattached from each other we pursue our own paths. Thus the bonhomie that existed during the war years, when everyone, out of necessity, stood shoulder to shoulder, had a shared goal and mutual common purpose, has been replaced in 21st century Britain by an uneasy tension, a daily conflict of personal and corporate interests.

Rights in conflict with responsibilities. Nameless economists in conflict with stable homes and strong communities. Parents in conflict with each other and their children. Exam laden pupils in conflict with 'results' laden teachers. Neighbour in conflict with neighbour (except in emergencies). Ethnic background and creed in conflict with ethnic background and creed. Disaffected, disillusioned, boundary less, nihilistic, often fatherless, sometimes violent young people in conflict with everyone. Reforming zeal in public services in conflict with reorganisation fatigue. Performance in conflict with cooperation. Politician in conflict with politician. Regrettably, the encouragement of competition and individual achievement into every area of life during the 1980s, 90s and early 21st century, has only sought to heighten that conflict. The rush to be 'first', 'top', 'highest paid', or 'most profitable', tending to set individuals or groups against each other. In the wake of our pursuit to be 'successful', we have lost the art of working together and enjoying relationship, our altruism towards others often being replaced with the question, 'But what's in it for me?'

Inside the home, this cancer of disconnection has been allowed to envelope the next generation, as children have frequently been discouraged from developing friendships by the condoning of an isolated, sedentary world in front of the laptop or P.C. Taking meals in front of the T.V. or in their bedrooms, thereby avoiding conversation and any form of intimacy. The 'home alone together' syndrome, where families are under the same roof but each in their own room, has thus unobtrusively been allowed to gain a foothold in our homes. Sue Palmer, author of *Toxic Childhood* comments,

'...in a world where opportunities for adults and children to talk together grow fewer and fewer, a regular shared meal is the ideal opportunity for chatting over the events of the day, swapping gossip and planning future activities. This type of social interaction cannot start too early, but as Karen Pasquali-Jones, editor of Mother and Baby magazine, has pointed out, as parents increasingly use television as an electronic babysitter, even toddlers are beginning to eat alone. As she says, 'Toddlers need the experience of sitting up at a table. It not only encourages them to eat properly; it improves their speech and social skills and encourages them to try new foods.

At the other end of the range, researchers at the University of Minnesota found that the more frequently teenagers ate with their parents, the less likely they were to smoke, drink, use marijuana, or show signs of depression.'

Palmer concludes,

'It doesn't take a rocket scientist to recognize that regular family get-togethers have a socializing and civilizing effect on children of all ages.'
Television of course cannot be entirely blamed for encouraging this isolation of relationships, but it is a key element. A time filler that

discourages rapport between real people in the real world. A diversion from engaging with others face to face. A diversion within the home that deters people from spending meaningful time together. Michael Schluter and David Lee in their book *The R Factor* make the situation clear,

> *'Watching TV is in the end an individual activity engaged in by individuals. You don't need other people. Their presence can enhance or spoil your enjoyment, according to circumstance; but you don't need them.'*

They conclude,

> *'We watch TV instead of going out. We watch TV instead of inviting friends in. We watch TV instead of talking.'*

It takes time to build relationships. Relationship building is therefore economically inefficient, requires commitment and can be inconvenient. It is relationships though that hold people, communities and nations together and without them life is empty. In the UK we have largely become, both inside and outside the home, a nation of 'private' people, viewing others only as participant competitors in the race of life, their needs being a nuisance, a constraint, an unwelcome obligation on what we want to achieve. We feel our focus must be on freeing ourselves from any responsibilities we might have towards other people and pursuing what is in our own best interests, in any way that suits us, provided we don't obstruct others in their pursuit of the same. Thus the 'Battle for Britain' has continued. And at present we are loosing it.

The Road to Nowhere

Although a national sense of disconnection from each other cannot be the responsibility of any one particular government, the situation has been exacerbated by successive administrations becoming disconnected from the very people they are seeking to govern, piling election promises on top of each other in an effort to 'out-bid' the competition, but not underpinning those promises with a coherent set of values. To avoid anarchy, though, every society needs to adhere to a common set of shared values. We need, therefore, values that rise above today's 'sound bite' or tomorrows 'big idea'. Values that everyone understands because they reflect the true nature of people. Values that give every individual self-worth and which encourage them to make a contribution to their local community. Values that can be applied with consistency to policy and practice. Values that reflect Britain's Judaeo-Christian heritage. Values that people instinctively adhere to thereby engendering a sense of national identity, for the truth is, countries that have no national identity often split into warring factions. Values that offer a vision for the future.

In the long-term, a government with an incoherent set of values is a government with no sense of direction. A government with no sense of direction is a government with no future. A government with no future ultimately leads to a nation with no hope. If the United Kingdom is to make lasting progress, its citizens need to have an idea of where they are going and why. To answer the question that Nick Spencer poses in his book *Votewise*, *'What, exactly, do we want as a society?'*

Do we really want to stay where we are, go back to where we were or initiate change in order to move society forward?

Most of the answers to most of the questions about which direction to go in, lie somewhere in-between the political parties, with each holding a piece of the puzzle but with no one having the complete picture. And, with limited opportunity for cross party cooperation, no real likelihood of the puzzle ever being completed.

Regrettably the electorate are prevented from assisting in that political cooperation, as constituents are currently prisoners of an archaic voting system that not only allows one party to govern without consultation, cross party consent and often without a majority of the popular vote, but also never allows the high ideals of opposition parties to be tested. Thus, whilst some electors have enjoyed a monopoly of power by their own particular party, others have suffered frustration, resentment and disillusionment, many choosing to disengage, not from an interest in politics, but from taking part in the election process. In March 2009, Polly Toynbee writing about proportional representation commented,

'The last election swung on just 200,000 votes in a handful of marginals. The derelict first-past-the-post electoral system leaves the nation's fate to a tiny proportion of the politically indifferent, disenfranchising everyone

else. Crass election messages try to catch the fleeting attention of a few bored people, the only ones that matter.

A proportional system means every vote counts, no longer piled up in safe seats or wasted hopeless seats. The two near memberless old parties have the system stitched up and voters are on strike. Tony Blair won just 25% of the electorate in 2005. Mrs Thatcher turned the country hard right, yet never had a majority, as Conservatives dominated the last century, despite a social democratic majority.'

She concludes,

'A promise to break the system and let new parties flourish, gaining votes according to popularity, working in coalitions better weighted to the popular vote would show a new trust in the electorate.'

In the long-term, domination by one person, or one party, can only undermine democracy, as people acknowledge that their vote for an alternative political party is valueless and domination tends to encourage arrogance.

The collective outcome of this political malaise is that currently the United Kingdom is not governed by a parliament but ruled by a system. The war has thus continued as, once in power, politicians from the ruling party can choose to ignore other points of view and press ahead with their own legislative programme generally frustrating the will of the majority of the electorate. Party politics has come to mean that its adherents have a divided loyalty between the party or those they represent, often with the party having the greatest influence, the good of the country taking second place to the good of the coterie.

The agenda of the party conference being not, 'Will the wisdom of these policies be applauded by the next generation?' but, 'How can our party win another term in office?' Strong government is only ever achieved when those in power are supported by the majority of the electorate. Without the consent of the majority, it is always the few imposing their will on the many.

No one party alone, can ever be flexible enough to respond adequately to the challenges of a rapidly changing world. Varied problems require a variety of solutions and no single party or person can ever have the monopoly on wisdom. For this nation to flourish we need cross-fertilisation in government, not self-justification. There is strength in unity, beauty in diversity. But wisdom comes from shared opinion.

There is no shortage of ideas in the United Kingdom. It is common consent and a structure to practically realise them that is lacking. Problems of the 21st century will not be resolved by a 19th century political system and a 20th century view of the world.

If this nation truly desires to be at peace with itself and for its people to reconnect with each other, there must be political change. There must be a move away from democratic dictatorship and the domination of single party government. For the essence of a peaceful society is power with, not power over. Regrettably, the current electoral system only encourages those in power to become so detached from those they represent, their credibility is often undermined and their decisions distrusted. It is parliament itself, therefore, that needs to be reformed before changes can, without hypocrisy, be asked of other sections of society.

The citizens of England, Northern Ireland, Scotland and Wales have the right to expect that government at both national and local level will be of the highest quality, cost- effective, efficient and sensitive to the needs of those it serves. To bring peace to the United Kingdom and calm to a turbulent world, therefore, it is *wise* local and national government that is now required. Government that fosters a unity amongst its people similar to that forged during the 'world-war' years. It is only wise government that can provide lasting stability and lead the nation adroitly towards the end of time. A stability that is attained by only ever needing to gently adjust the tiller by planned review, rather than continually rocking the boat by enforced U turns or crisis led interventions. We have become so used to adequate government that we have forgotten what excellent government looks like.

The Road Forward

The key for the future, then, is not so much having the right political Party in power, but the right people, those who can construct a framework of policy within a coherent set of values against which many of today's complex issues can be considered; those who are willing to lay aside individual Party preferences and work together as one. Successive governments have often become responders to problems as they arise, rather than developing foresight and initiating creative responses in order to achieve enduring resolutions before a crisis occurs. They have become adept at closing the door after the horse has bolted and then blaming the horse for escaping.

If leadership of a nation is about anything, it must be about seeking to anticipate the demands of the future by listening to those who live in the real world and making the necessary provision, rather than pursuing short-term, short-sighted options and leaving someone else to inherit the problems.

Ultimately, national peace and prosperity will not be achieved by slick election promises but by perceptive government for a generation. Government that understands the difference between the reality of living on the frontline of life and wishful electioneering. It takes courage to step away from taking those decisions that are politically expedient, but it takes a greater courage to listen to those with whom we may not agree. For there is sometimes a grain of truth in the words of even those seen as having extreme views.

To criticise those in power is not difficult, as is never admitting you are wrong. Far more could be achieved, however, if those men and women elected as Members of Parliament worked together. Patience, respect and understanding need again to be seen as strengths not weaknesses.

"I apologise to no one", has no place in a nation seeking to foster amity. A nation that wants to champion the case for democracy across the world needs first to live at one with itself. To be a nation that is heterogeneous, but whose people have a common sense of purpose.

We cannot turn the clock back, but neither does this nation have to be a hostage to foolish legislation. Neither does everything need to be changed. For, where some progress has been achieved the opportunity to build upon it needs to be pursued.

Our need then, as a nation, is not to get 'back to basics', but to move on from the current level of political staleness. The problem being that governments not so much 'lose the plot' but, by losing contact with real people, they completely forget what the play is about. Consequently government policies are often part of the problem, not part of the solution.

Government and public life is about more than 'obeying the rules' or blaming the system when misdemeanours are highlighted. It is about

MAURICE JONES

morality. It is about values. It is about having an innate sense of knowing when and where to draw the line.

At this moment in history, therefore, the United Kingdom needs men and women as leaders who are ready to listen, ready to care for those in need, ready to honourably fulfil their parliamentary duties and to place the nations interests before their own or their Party's. In short, politicians who want long-term solutions, not long-term power. Politicians who have the courage to tackle problems at their root, not further their own political career. Politicians who understand as much about ordinary people, as they do about the political system. Politicians who seek to achieve the balance between personal freedom/individual rights and collective responsibilities. Politicians who pursue common sense, not political correctness.

Politicians who acknowledge that wisdom comes from dialogue with others and their Creator. Politicians whose personal lives uphold the standards they ask of others and who seek themselves, along with others in high public office, to lead the nation by example.

Politicians who choose not to 'bury bad news', but are honest about their failings. Politicians who are not seduced themselves or seek to seduce others by engaging with the 'sultans of spin'. Politicians who respect their position of power and authority and seek, not to improve their own lives, but improve the lives of those they represent. For scandal in whatever form, within the House of Commons, distracts politicians from focussing on the life and death issues they are paid, by the taxpayer, to consider and act upon. We need then to replace confrontation with considered consensus and the sterility of one Party supremacy, with meaningful, constructive, 'grown-up' democracy, thereby creating a political process that encourages each one in the Houses of Commons and Lords to work alongside the other.

We need then, to challenge and change our entire political system, so as to ensure the sole ambition of those who would seek to lead the United Kingdom in the years ahead will be to practise, in word and deed, both humility and service.

CHAPTER TWO

Working Together

*'So we rebuilt the wall till all of it reached half its height,
for the people worked with all their heart.'*

Nehemiah 4:6

Since the 1960s many institutions in the United Kingdom have experienced a radical reshaping. However, like many social experiments, often what you are left with is not necessarily an improvement on what you had before. In recent days, 'new' has not automatically meant 'better'. Every nation needs to progress and develop and that inevitably means change. Change is only of lasting value however, when it is introduced gradually and with people's consent. Change that is forced not only breeds resentment, alienation and lethargy but also removes 'ownership' from those affected by the changes which, in time, destroys people's goodwill and thereby stifles initiative. At the very least, imposed change takes the fun out of life. It is people who are a nation's greatest asset. They are always the best investment and governments, therefore, need to ensure that when change is inaugurated, it is fully funded and meets people's needs. There have to be priorities, but priorities need to be agreed by consensus. For unless a nation is moving forward together it is not moving forward at all. It is either stagnating, or worse, in decline.

Real Prosperity

We are one nation and, as such, all have a vested interest and responsibility to help the United Kingdom become prosperous to the benefit of our neighbours and ourselves. Real prosperity, however, is only achieved when people's expectations are held in balance with their real requirements and consideration is given to other cogent issues. The mantra, 'unrestrained economic growth is always good' has masked the fact that the environmental costs of growth are beginning to outweigh the social and economic benefits. The question needs to be asked therefore, is unfettered global capitalism a part of the solution or a part of the problem? The truth is a market economy is only a good servant if it operates within a value-driven system, if it operates in a moral vacuum it becomes a very bad master. Unfettered and devoid of a moral context capitalism is ultimately destructive. The future demands therefore that people move on from the excesses of consumerism and materialism and endeavour to work out, in their daily living, what it means to enjoy a balanced and sustainable lifestyle, to begin to endorse an economic strategy that seeks to release all people from the bondage of poverty and riches.

To appreciate that pursuing an ever higher standard of living will, in the long-term, be as empty for themselves as it will be damaging for others. For we have become mesmerised by the illusion that an ever higher standard of living equates to an ever higher quality of life and that greed, either corporate or personal, can ever fulfil our deepest desires. Any government, therefore, whose overriding goal is to increase economic wealth at whatever the cost and considers 'progress' only in terms of economic growth and individual prosperity, has seriously misunderstood the varied needs of human beings.

Indeed when a government promotes the deception that the most important thing in a person's life is how much money they have in their pocket, then 'The economy, stupid', as one of Bill Clinton's aides once said, simply becomes, 'The stupid economy'.

The plain fact is that although in recent years people have generally been getting richer, they have not been getting happier and for some, the disease of the idolatry of affluence is now manifesting itself in stress, obesity, debt and depression.

In particular, the difficulty in managing work-life balance has, for many, put pressure on relationships and caused a feeling of disengagement from society. Its effect on parenting/ motherhood/fatherhood is an area that has proved especially problematic. In an economy focussed world, for some, their young children have become, at best, a restriction on earning ability. Elaine Storkey comments,

> 'Our society does not really know what it feels about parenting. On the one hand it sees the role as something anyone can do, on the other there are fewer than ever who seem prepared to take it on. In regular surveys the trends among young women have been marked. More and more of them say that they intend to stay childless. Their reasons are interesting. Many feel that having children is incompatible with the demands they already have to meet within their present life-style, and this is the only life-style they can envisage. Born into small families, where their mothers were working by the time they were teenagers, many young women have not seen parenting at first hand, or known the stay-at-home patterns of an earlier generation. So, having children and bringing them up has become for many the great unknown. And people who are skilled in the workplace can quickly feel deskilled when faced with a job of full-time nurturing.'

Storkey continues,

> 'But there is also the status of mothers. Sadly it is low. Many mothers of young babies who had once held down highly respected jobs now feel marginalised when asked the inevitable question, 'What do you do?' They hate the answer 'I'm just a housewife' because of course they are not. Housewifery, along with parenting is a job which calls for multiple skills, problem solving and time management, as any of those who have made it their profession will admit. It is a job where there are no set hours, and where overtime is inevitable and unpaid. Those who benefit from equal rights in the workplace are reluctant to give that up for very unequal rights in the home.'

She concludes,

> 'I believe that at the heart of our crisis over parenting lies, not feminism, but its devaluation within society as a whole. And at the heart of that lies an alternative system of values: a relentless consumerism that redefines our life and our worth. People become work machines, time is money, choice is sacrosanct and individual freedom is the highest value. A Christian

perspective has to work hard to have its voice heard. We have to demonstrate that motherhood is a high and dignified calling. Even more, we have to show that fatherhood is too.'

When market capitalism with its attendant focus on self-interest, self-gratification and consequent selfishness is given free rein, society goes into free fall, as any activity or person considered 'uneconomic' is viewed as being of doubtful value. Also, when we are persuaded by market capitalism that our 'wants' are really 'needs' then our focus is diverted away from helping or showing an interest in others, onto our own self-fulfilment, our self-centredness making us introvert, impatient and complaining.

In that environment, as Roy McCloughry explains, market capitalism has no problem in justifying its existence and becoming a self-fulfilling prophecy.

'The market, we are now told, 'is meeting needs'. Yet it is the market which is also creating those needs. In the midst of this, contentment is discarded as a virtue.'

Thus, by encouraging discontent, market capitalism creates a void to fill and thereby ensures its own survival. At its root, capitalism is principally about encouraging people to buy things they don't need with money they haven't got.

We need therefore to admit that our national loss of community and consequent disconnection has stemmed, in part, from our desire to earn enough to 'shop till we drop', thereby leaving our homes empty during the day, our streets devoid of social contact and our communities devoid of anybody who has 'spare time' to talk or help those who are socially isolated, elderly or immobile.

Occasional 'retail therapy' may be beneficial, but in a nation where loneliness is a significant problem, maybe 'people therapy' needs to be more fully embraced. Likewise, escaping into a world where semi-virtual people strike up semi-virtual relationships with other semi-virtual people may pass the time of day, but it does little to help us gain satisfaction from engaging with real people, in the real world.

David Derbyshire comments,

> 'Living in a community with a thriving Women's Institute, busy charity shop and active church choir is good for the health, a major study claims. Researchers have found that neighbourhoods with the highest levels of voluntary work have less crime, better schools and happier, healthier residents than districts without community spirit.

> "Communities with lots of volunteering tend to be communities where people are very satisfied with their lives," said Prof Paul Whitely, who led the study. "It seems that when we focus on the needs of others, we may also reap benefits ourselves."

The creation of wealth in itself is not wrong, and nations need to earn their prosperity rather than borrow it, so that the next generation is not born into debt. The fair, just and wise distribution of that prosperity however, rests on the shoulders of government. The problem in recent years has not been a shortage of money to spend, but a list of priorities that have owed more to political manoeuvring than community building. An individual's desire to be innovative in commerce, industry or everyday life, needs to be motivated by more than a desire just to create wealth. For, it is a deception to believe that an increase in personal or national wealth is a good measure of the overall well-being of an individual or a nation. Robert Kennedy, speaking in 1968, made it clear that economic output alone was far too narrow a measure for assessing a nation's well-being.

> 'Too much and too long, we seem to have surrendered community excellence and community values in the mere accumulation of material things … Gross national product does not allow for the health of our children, the quality of their education, or the joy of their play. It does not include the beauty of our poetry or the strength of our marriages; the intelligence of our public debate or the integrity of our public officials. It measures neither our wit nor our courage; neither our wisdom nor our learning; neither our compassion nor our devotion to our country; it measures everything, in short, except that which makes life worthwhile.'

Created wealth needs to be wisely invested in improving existing facilities or initiating new projects. For wealth creation is only of lasting value when, like a river, it can flow in a direction that will ultimately benefit a multitude. Without an outlet, wealth simply becomes stagnant and loses its meaning. The issue is not, 'How much wealth can I create?' but, 'What am I creating it for?' Wealth that is only redistributed amongst a select few is like pouring clean water into the Dead Sea. Thus it is not wealth creation but the love of the money we create that is problematical. What needs urgent consideration then is what we choose to do with our wealth.

Any nation that is seeking to encourage a benevolent attitude amongst its inhabitants, needs to reflect that an increase in personal affluence must always be equalled by an increase in personal responsibility.

Personal charitable giving can be of value, but dipping into your pocket to support a television appeal or street collection, although worthwhile, is not enough. For it is not the amount we give that is important, but our attitude to people on the other 364 days of the year. Becoming a donating society is a noble aim but, unless the contributions demonstrate something of a sacrifice by the individuals concerned, it offers little long-term benefit to the recipient and little long-term satisfaction to the donor. One thing is certain, real compassion is never cheap. For often those who are the most vulnerable are the most expensive to maintain and the first to suffer when resources are limited.

It is true that money is necessary in most societies. It is also true, however, that the best things in life are free. Thus, when personal gain is an individual's only reason for working or living, everyone loses.

Public Service and Private Enterprise

Natural competition in some areas of life is healthy, for it can provide stimulation and an incentive to achieve our best, by using our talents more creatively. Unbridled and imposed, however, it can destroy initiative and stimulate a 'survival of the fittest' attitude amongst those whose only goal is to win at whatever the cost.

Such an overriding attitude can have no place in a society that is seeking to move forward not back, a society that is seeking social cohesion. There may be some satisfaction in winning your own particular race, but it also needs to be recognised that coming second or third or last can be just as worthwhile provided some progress is achieved. It may be the case that, in the world of commerce and industry, increased competition is one way of improving efficiency and thereby cutting costs. It is also true however, that greater productivity and quality of service, can be achieved by a highly motivated workforce, who enjoy job satisfaction and job security, which tends to be more beneficial in human terms and also means an organisation does not necessarily have to be run as a 'ruthlessly competitive business' to be effective.

Employees in the private sector should always want to give of their best, not because of financial inducements, but because of a satisfaction in knowing they have created an end product of high quality. Likewise, employers need to acknowledge that positive relationships within the workplace not only relieve stress and absenteeism, but greatly increase the contribution made by the employee, which can be commercially advantageous to a company when it leads to enhanced relationships with customers and suppliers. The best way then, to obtain meaningful efficiency in any business, is to ensure that those who are seeking to work efficiently feel that they are valued and that they are achieving something that will be beneficial and appreciated; that their worth as a person is not solely dependent upon what performance target they can reach; and that their loyalty to the company will be reciprocated by the company being loyal to them when decisions are being made. Downsizing, reorganising or outsourcing may improve a company's balance sheet and maximise the dividend paid to shareholders, but when staff forfeit their employment without their employer giving due regard to the employees future, greed has triumphed over humanity.

Richard Donkin writing in the *Financial Times* expresses,

'... *treating people well should be fundamental to all areas of employment. It doesn't need a trendy description such as "engagement", just good manners and mutual respect.*'

Thus, if compulsory redundancy is ever a company's prime or only means of improving competitiveness, they have already lost the battle to maintain human dignity. Competition certainly has no place in the public sector. For the government of the day should be seeking to enhance the concept of 'public service', not degrade it, seeking to enable the public services to become organizational role models of how people can work together.

It is not league tables that are needed to improve services, but an assumption that those providing the services will naturally give of their best, because their instinctive desire is to work in collaboration in order to better assist those whom they are seeking to serve. In the public domain therefore, honest appreciation, respect and trust need to be used to increase individual effort, not divisive performance-related pay awards, or the pressurising of public servants by the raising of unrealistic expectations in the general public with regard to what the public services can deliver, or the offering of fanciful rights/entitlements/guarantees to the public without the resources to match the demand, or the pursuit of counter-productive target setting regimes that have pitted professionals against each other. Neither has privatisation a place in a non-competitive Public Sector. Privatisation, by its very nature, is divisive, dislocates services and takes responsibility away from government by placing it in the hands of individual shareholders and private companies whose first priority may, or may not be, the general well-being of the nation or its citizens. Also, when work is subcontracted the chain of responsibility becomes ever more tenuous. All public services need to be accountable to elected representatives, thereby ensuring the electorate is always the final arbiter in how the services are provided and the sole beneficiary. Public services do not exist to make a profit. They exist to serve the nation. Some utilities may create enough revenue to allow for development by reinvestment. Some services, like schools and hospitals, need to be totally funded from the public purse, thereby enjoying the stability of guaranteed long-term financial support.

To invest in public services from the public purse, then, is not wasteful, for the money needs to be seen as an investment in people, many of whom, over the years, will substantially repay the initial outlay.

There is of course no value in using public money to maintain a service or organisation that needs to alter or stop altogether. But, as a parent has a continuing responsibility to invest in their child in order to bring them to a well-rounded maturity, so likewise, governments have the same responsibility to invest public money in public services for the lasting benefit of us all. Ultimately then, governments need to work in partnership with industry and commerce to everyone's advantage, with each knowing where the boundaries of the public and private sector lie. Businesses cannot have it both ways. In boom times, the business community calls for low taxes, minimal regulation and limited government intervention. However in bust times businesses call for maximum government intervention via financial bail-outs. Businesses, like everyone else, need to achieve the balance between independence and interdependence. Industry and commerce need to be vibrant and profitable, not only to provide a modest remuneration for their shareholders, but also to reinvest in their own future and the future of the nation by helping to finance the public sector for everyone's benefit.

There is, of course, a place for those who may wish to spend their own money on private education, healthcare or other services. But, in a society rightly balanced between individual and collective rights and responsibilities, a government's priority is to ensure the provision of amply resourced public services for the benefit of the nation as a whole. In sum, government needs to promote public investment and encourage private enterprise in equal measure.

Wise Management

Simply spending more and more public money on public services, however, cannot solve all the problems. Higher spending has to go hand in hand with wise, effective and considerate administration.

Waste, in any sphere of life, public or private, be it in terms of human or natural resources, can never be justified, and always results from a mixture of poor management and wrong attitudes or simply having too much. It is easy though to lay the blame at someone else's door, when in fact we all have a responsibility not to waste resources and to ensure that what is already available is always used to the full. However, those who hold positions of influence at all levels of local and national government need to be held particularly responsible for achieving the balance between sound budgeting, social justice, minimising bureaucracy and avoiding money wastage. In that way taxes will always be wisely spent.

UK United

The bottom line then, in these early days of the 21st century, is not only does the United Kingdom need to change the way it is governed, but also it needs a change of direction. The future direction of this nation, however, lies not with the government, but with each one of us, young or old, rich or poor, whatever our ethnic background. And progress will only be achieved when we, as individuals, all participate in that process. We need to move beyond seeing a person in terms of their background, what they do, what they own, their colour or creed, and value people for who they are. To remind ourselves that it is not how an individual looks that is important, but the person inside that matters. To re-examine our sometimes preconceived negative opinions about others, in order to discover their true source and to see ourselves and others as whole, three-dimensional people. For the majority of human behaviour cannot be quantified and neatly packaged. Not that we necessarily condone the conduct of those we may meet, watch or hear about, but we embrace them simply because they are fellow human beings. For, not all 'hoodies' are criminals. Not all criminals are beyond reform. Not all who are different from us are our enemies. We need also to appreciate that neither technology nor economics will ever give all the answers to life's problems but that they will become our master rather than our slaves, without proper direction and our maturity in their use. Direction that comes from the heart as well as the head. For true wisdom has little to do with the pure acquisition of knowledge. We need to recall that no man or woman was ever meant to be an island. Independence is important, but only leads to the boredom of self-centred living if individuals are not rooted in a wider community. There is no escape. Like it or not, every individual action has an effect on someone else. We cannot and neither should we be seeking to escape from the rest of the world. Escapism may have its place, but disengagement leads to a barrenness of the soul and a hardness of the heart.

Caring about others has nothing to do with age, financial status or intellectual ability.

It is simply a part of what it means to be human. Charity towards others is not an 'optional extra', but a commitment we are bequeathed by virtue of the fact we are all born alike and all share the same planet. Thus, my 'humanness' is debased when I turn my back on the needy. Self-absorption may bring personal satisfaction, but it will not bring personal fulfilment. I only begin to be complete as a human being, when I begin to embrace others. What defines my personhood is not how much I own, but how much I give. Serving others, in whatever way, in whatever sphere, is not a sign of weakness but of inner strength. Self-centred behaviour is a sign of insecurity, a demonstration of low self-esteem and a lack of self-confidence. As a society, therefore, we need to encourage a sense of community wherever we live, a sense of interdependency. Our homes are not mini 'banana republics'. Disengagement with our neighbours deprives them and ourselves of a sense of belonging, a sense of mutual understanding of our own unique story, a sense of mutual respect and an offering of mutual care.

We need to rediscover within our community the pleasure of giving 'something for nothing', to offer compassion rather than pity to those in need as, in reality, from time to time we are all in need, but we are not always honest enough to admit it. We can choose to ignore people, but the time may come when, to our detriment, they choose to ignore us. The essence of community, be it in town, city or village, is that everyone contributes for the good of everyone else. That we give as well as receive and thereby fulfil our joint responsibilities towards each other. I am happy to discharge my responsibility of contributing towards the cost of your healthcare, provided you undertake to maintain as healthy a lifestyle as possible. You are willing to contribute towards the cost of my child's education, provided I ensure their attendance and good behaviour. I am willing to fund your university placement, provided you spend more time in the lecture theatre than in the bar. Conversely, your tax-haven/tax-fraud is my hospital waiting list. My black market is your leaking classroom. Your choice not to work is someone else's benefit reduction. Your cheap flight and my three minute drive to the shops, is our climate change and our grandchildren's worst nightmare. Our cut-price food is a million animal's miserable existence. My cheap clothing is someone else's cheap labour. One nation's prosperity is often another nation's poverty. Thus our individual 'rights' always need to be balanced by our responsibilities to others. Always.

We therefore need to re-engage with each other locally, nationally

MAURICE JONES

and internationally, to promote responsibility expressed through decisive action.

A change of direction in society is always best sustained when it is complemented by the example of those in leadership. If I am encouraged by government to 'look after number one', I will soon lose respect for other people and their property. Our political system, therefore, needs to undergo major reforms so that a greater cohesion can be achieved in every area of national life.

Not that democracy in whatever form will solve all of a nation's difficulties, but a future built on individuals working collectively will always achieve more than individuals working alone.

Although the British parliament is called the 'Mother of all Parliaments', it has, over the years, failed to acknowledge that although some parliamentary traditions are of value, society overall has changed and the electorate now desire parliament to reflect those changes. Adversarial politics therefore have no place in the 21st century. Consensual politics that encourage wise debate must be the future if the United Kingdom is ever going to be just that. United. In any society seeking to moderate the excesses of individualism and subdue the seduction of self-determination at the expense of others, the onus on people is to 'opt in', not 'opt out'. Fragmentation, ghetto-isation, closure of local services and the loss of local governance will never engender national unanimity, nor assist in promoting a coherent national programme of reconstruction and reconnection. You cannot legislate your way to a harmonious society. Bombarding people with rules, regulations and edicts usually results in apathy. But if attitudes can be changed by encouraging people to open their hearts and their minds, then the future can be one of real progress. A new dawn. An end to hostilities.

With a nation, as with any individual, the past does not have to determine your future. It is possible to break the mould. Indeed, often the hard part is not removing the old structure, it is having the enthusiasm and imagination to build a new one. The future can be what we make it. But we need to start soon. For only when this process of change has been commenced, will the United Kingdom be on its way to achieving hope for the future, justice, forgiveness, reconciliation, meaningful prosperity and lasting peace.

CHAPTER THREE

A Step in the Right Direction

*'In everything you do, put God first, and he will direct you
and crown your efforts with success.'*

Proverbs 3:6

What then is God's heart for the United Kingdom? What is His manifesto for social and political change? What policies need to be put into place to begin the process of healing?

If we define the essentials of democracy as being: equality before the law and trial by jury; freedom of conscience and religion/belief expressed through teaching, practice, worship and observance; freedom to change ones religion/belief; individual freedom of choice to wear religious clothing/symbols unless it contravenes Health and Safety regulations or the dress code of certain public institutions i.e. schools/hospitals/police; freedom of thought and expression; absence of arbitrary arrest and detention; the protection of citizens from state oppression such as murder, torture and imprisonment; individual autonomy within the confines of the law; the dignity, value and equal status of women and men; the protection of privacy and property from arbitrary interference and confiscation; action against public corruption; reasonable tolerance in all areas of life and the right to vote in a way where every vote is valued, and that we, as individuals, want to live in a democracy and share those 'essentials' with other nations without being hypocritical, it is important that we put them fully into practice. So where do we start?

Central Government

Determining the lives of others is a privilege and an awesome responsibility. In order to be truly representative, Members of Parliament need to live as much as possible in the 'real world' and spend time listening to their constituents, those with a different perspective and their own feelings. Above all, however, they need to be men and women of high standing within their local community. Men and women of integrity who are willing to work together for the common good. Men and women who see their position in the House of Commons not as a career, but as a vocation.

Men and women drawn from across the nation, for there is no such thing as the 'West Lothian question'. On questions of national and international importance, wise answers are required that are forged from national wisdom, wisdom that has been accumulated by Members of Parliament drawn from the full spectrum of life.

Scotland, Wales and Northern Ireland all have a rich cultural heritage and a proud past. History and geography, however, have combined to make England, Northern Ireland, Scotland and Wales more than 'near neighbours'. The life of every inhabitant has been inextricably woven together by historic events and shared experience. The uncertainties of the future require a drawing from that well of collective experience and a unity that sacrifices individual nationalism for shared foresight, a unity that seeks to learn from and blend together the best of each nation.

For many years successive governments have seen their primary task as increasing economic output and encouraging material gain. That narrow focus, however, has not only impoverished the lives of people in other ways, it has also abused the environment. It is critical therefore that all future legislation is considered in terms of its social, economic and environmental impact.

Democracy is precious. Defending it has, over the years, been costly. It is therefore important that central government promotes democracy at every level within the United Kingdom and encourages its establishment (albeit in other forms) around the world.

*   All Members of Parliament to be elected by a system of proportional

representation that enables the will of the people to be represented in Parliament in proportion to how they have voted, retains single member constituencies, has a minimum threshold of votes that avoids fringe parties creating unstable coalitions and is easy for voters to understand. Each parliamentary term to last for a fixed five year period.

> 'The government has responded to falling turnouts with postal ballots and various schemes such as voting outside supermarkets. We have grave concerns about the potential for increased levels of electoral fraud. Greens believe in a more radical approach, with a system that more accurately reflects local opinion, reduces the power of marginal seats and breaks the sterile grip of the two-party system. The Green Party will therefore continue to campaign for proportional representation for Westminster elections.'
> (Green Party Election Manifesto 2005 p.27)

★   The Prime Minister to remain in post for no more than two terms. MPs to remain in post for no more than five terms.

★   Parliamentary day to be reorganised in line with office hours and recesses in line with school holidays, so as to encourage a wider cross-section of men and women to become MPs. By-elections to be held within six weeks of an MPs resignation/death.

> 'The SSP stands for: Equal representation for women at all levels of government.'
> (Scottish Socialist Party Election Manifesto 2005 p.33)

★   MPs to live in the constituency they represent and drawn, where possible, from the locality. Minimum age 25 years.

★   House of Lords to be reformed so as to comprise a wider cross-section of men and women chosen from their local area by nomination and confirmed by a local election. Those elected to the House of Lords to remain in post for no more than two terms. Minimum age 50 years. House of Lords to remain a revising chamber.

> 'The House of Lords will be reformed to become a fully elected body ...'
> (Green Party Election Manifesto 2005, p.27)

★   The UK Supreme Court to be the highest court in the United Kingdom with no referral to the European Court.

★   Abolish the Assemblies of Northern Ireland, Wales and the Scottish Parliament. Local Government leaders in all parts of the United Kingdom to seek to preserve and promote national identity at a local level.

> 'The English are upset that Scots and Welsh MPs decide English policies and are concerned about the level of subsidy to Wales and Scotland.'
> (Veritas Election Manifesto 2005, Devolution)

★   Expenses of MPs and those sitting in the House of Lords to be agreed by an independent review body and claimed on the basis of being wholly necessary for an MP to effectively fulfil their function of representation. All claims to be independently audited, available for public scrutiny and based on the most cost effective viable alternative i.e. ending first-class travel.

All MPs who represent constituencies outside London to have access whilst they are in the capital to secure, fully furnished, fully serviced, state-owned accommodation.

All office staff i.e. secretary/PA to be provided by the Civil Service. Constituency offices used by an MP to carry out their parliamentary duties, to be fully funded by the state.

All MPs and those sitting in the House of Lords to be full-time, without pursuing outside business interests, maintaining second jobs or receiving payment for parliamentary services i.e. advocacy for lobby groups.

★   Cabinet ministers to have some knowledge or experience of the ministry to which they are appointed and to be drawn, whenever beneficial, from across the political spectrum and expected to remain in office for the full parliamentary term.

Central Government to have specific responsibility for defence, the economy, customs and excise, international trade, foreign policy, justice and overall responsibility for all other areas.

★   Government to encourage a cross-fertilisation of ideas and solutions at all levels of society.

*   Minimum voting age 18 years.

*   Quasi-autonomous non-governmental organisations are publicly funded and influential, yet unaccountable to the electorate. Review all quangos with a view to abolishment or revision.

*   Disestablish Church and state.

*   Maintain the monarchy as it currently exists, with the emphasis being on self-funding with a prudent increase in the Civil List, and the covering of expenses when members of the Royal family are on official business.

    To protect the integrity of the monarchy, encourage Prince Charles to allow his eldest son to succeed the Queen.

    Encourage respect for all those in positions of responsibility. Encourage those in positions of responsibility to live in such a way that earns them respect.

*   Initiate relational health audits in all government departments.

    'For ... the individual employee, it is the relationships at the office that make your work pleasant or intolerable. Overbearing bosses, office politics, bullying, sexual harassment, unhealthy competitiveness between individuals-all these are signs of dysfunction in relationships. And a mismanaged relational environment impacts directly on morale, motivation, and productivity.'
    (Michael Schluter and David John Lee)

*   Improve the level of government accountability by enhancing the Select Committee system and ensure the political neutrality of the Civil Service. The decision to engage British Forces in any armed conflict to be taken by the House of Commons. Encourage honest and open government and reject patronage in all its forms.

    'In recent decades Prime Ministers have exercised a growing domination over the political system, insufficiently accountable to Parliament or the people. We will curb this excessive concentration of power ... We will make the Royal Prerogative powers which the Prime Minister exercises-such as decisions over war and peace-subject to parliamentary accountability ...

We will also strengthen the powers of Parliament to scrutinise the actions of the Government, enhancing the Select Committee system.'
(Liberal Democrat Election Manifesto 2005, p.18)

⋆   To enable voters to reflect on the issues without undue pressure, ban all political advertising and polling one week prior to the day of a general election. All Parliamentary debates to be broadcast on radio, but reduce television coverage.

⋆   Substantially reduce private sector involvement in public services. Seek to restore the ethos of 'public service'. Public servants i.e. police, doctors/nurses to have a system of career progression that avoids the necessity to change jobs or move into management to progress. Those trained by the state to commit themselves to working in their particular profession for five years. National pay scales for all public sector workers i.e. MPs, teachers, NHS staff and police to be set by an Independent Pay Review Body and centrally funded. End performance-related pay/cash bonuses for all public/Civil Service workers and local authority council staff.

'Plaid Cymru ... will: Restore the morale of people working in the public services, reducing unnecessary bureaucracy, scrapping market mechanisms, mobilising the dedication and professionalism-the public services' greatest assets.'
(Plaid Cymru Election Manifesto 2005, p.9)

'The Green Party believes we must restore pride in our public services, re-emphasise the service ethos, increase their resources and free them from commercial management.' (Green Party Election Manifesto 2005, p.14)

Although Health and Safety is important in relation to all services provided by the state, excessive application is unrealistic and inhibitive. Whilst all reasonable care and attention must be taken, risk and human error are a fact of life and those using the services need to accept that only acts of deliberate negligence can ever be acknowledged. Investigations into allegations, therefore, against public servants, need to be unbiased, based on reasonable evidence and operate to a national code of practice.

Local Government

The prime function of local government is to provide essential, reasonably priced, quality services to those living within its boundaries and to be responsive to the needs of its local communities.

For this to occur, power needs to be devolved from Central Government to local government via all purpose Unitary District Councils and Parish Councils, thus creating a 'bottom up' democracy, so local people can easily contact their local representative to express their views and make their concerns known.

National standards need to be set so that disparities in level of service between councils is removed and local services need to be paid for by as fair a means as possible.

Also, Councillors need to be men and women of high standing within their local community, men and women of integrity who are willing to work together for the common good.

★   Abolish the post of Mayor of London.

★   Abolish all forms of regional government and return their powers and responsibilities to local government.

> *'Conservatives understand that people identify with their town, city or county, not with arbitrary "regions". We will abolish…regional assemblies. Powers currently exercised at a regional level covering planning, housing, transport and the fire service will all be returned to local authorities.'*
> (Conservative Party Election Manifesto 2005, p.21)

★   Local government to be administered by Unitary District Councils based on existing districts within existing counties. All Unitary District Councillors to be elected by a system of proportional representation. Minimum age 25 years.

Extend the powers of Parish Councils. Parish councillors to be elected by a system of proportional representation. Minimum age 25 years. Encourage candidates for local council seats from as wide a cross-section of the local community as possible.

'Recruitment of candidates for local council seats from as wide a range as possible of the local population.'
(Plaid Cymru Election Manifesto 2005, p.14)

★ All expenses claimed by councillors in pursuit of their duties to be independently audited, available for public scrutiny and based on cost-effectiveness. Cap the pay of local government Chief Executive Officers.

★ Local government to be financed by a local income tax.

'A Local Income Tax is based very simply on the ability to pay. It would be run through the existing Inland Revenue Income Tax mechanism, so saving hundreds of millions of pounds by abolishing Council Tax administration.'
(Liberal Democrat Election Manifesto 2005, p.12-13)

'Many public services are provided by local authorities, which also make important planning decisions and have an important role as representatives of local people. It is essential that these functions are carried out by councils which are fully equipped for these tasks and command public respect. Plaid Cymru … believes that this requires - the abolition of council tax and its replacement by local income tax.'
(Plaid Cymru Election Manifesto 2005, p.14)

★ Local councillors to have responsibility within their geographical area for electoral registration, all planning issues, housing, archives, consumer protection, healthcare promotion, police, fire service, roads, allotments, cemeteries and crematoria, tourism/recreation and art, personal social services/personal care provision, residential/community care, emergency planning, employees pensions, highways, environmental services, public transport, registration of births/deaths etc. libraries, the general promotion of economic development and, to local businesses, advice and the opportunity to tender for council projects (but not offering direct financial support), and the monitoring/planning of education and healthcare delivery.

Strategic needs and promotion of a county as a whole, to be

considered by a County Planning Group, comprising of the leaders of each Unitary District Council.

Unitary District Councils to work in mutual collaboration with regard to all services and avoid duplication of council posts. Counties to work in mutual collaboration with other counties/local Members of Parliament/government ministers, so as to disperse good practice and ensure services are provided with equality across the United Kingdom.

Local government, whilst being responsible for providing many basic services, to support innovative projects run by charities and the voluntary sector and ensure they have access to decision makers in the public sector. Encourage charities to work together.

> *'The voluntary sector plays a crucial role in providing direct services, in innovating and experimenting, in mobilising public concern and willingness to help out, in strengthening local community life, and in putting forward policy ideas. Plaid Cymru will continue to support the work of the voluntary sector, and to help ensure it has access to decision-makers in the public sector.'*
> (Plaid Cymru Election Manifesto 2005 p.9)

Economy

It is the responsibility of the Government to ensure stability in the financial sector through monitoring and regulation.

For an economy to be balanced and sustainable in the long-term, it needs to be based on the export of goods, services, financial expertise and creative enterprises rather than consumer led and fed by imports fuelled by debt. The 'credit crunch' has exposed the imprudence of recent UK government monetary policy and the willingness to 'privatise' wealth in the good times and 'socialise' debt in the bad times is not an example of sound financial acumen, but a demonstration of lop-sided financial management and desperation, rather than careful consideration. Debt in all its forms, unless it is for investment, may provide short-term benefit if managed properly, but in the long-term because of the level of repayments it is financially inefficient. Governments therefore must live within their means and encourage others to do so. It is the responsibility of high street banks to guarantee the deposits of their savers and avoid financial insecurity through reckless corporate lending and encouraging high levels of personal borrowing. It is also the responsibility of venture capitalists, whilst working in a free market, to operate separately from high street banks, at their own risk and within the law.

Stability, particularly of interest rates, is essential, both for those planning to invest in industry and the individual planning his/her budget. Also, tax rates need to be set at a level that encourages everyone to contribute to provide high quality public services for themselves and their neighbour and to assist those who are on low incomes to work without being penalised. As tax evasion, either corporate or personal, deprives everyone else of necessary services, every attempt should be made to reduce the problem, particularly those earning high salaries who may be able to take advantage of tax relief and other means of avoiding tax liabilities. The truth is, we should not work (either paid or unpaid) to simply fulfil our own needs, but also the needs of the society within which we live. We need a change of attitude. Tax, particularly on those with high incomes, is not a punishment we strive to avoid. It is a social obligation. It is not an act of largesse. It is a symbol of citizenship. There is no less of a responsibility on those talented people who work hard for a modest remuneration and those talented people who work hard and receive higher salaries, to pay their taxes. 'Opting out' for either group is not an option.

Taxation not only has economic repercussions, but also social repercussions in many areas that need to be fully taken into consideration. For instance, the financial cost to the taxpayer of family breakdown is substantial. Taxation in this area therefore, although not a panacea, should be used to encourage couples to stay together. Monetary policy and tax incentives then should be focussed on enabling industry and commerce to invest in long-term employment, the export of their goods and services and seeking creative opportunities during economic downturn to sow the seeds of economic recovery. Often in an economic slowdown, companies are tempted to ignore 'green' or 'sustainable' initiatives to reduce costs. However, maintaining these initiatives can in fact be the most effective way of reducing costs. Cutting waste to landfill sites, improving manufacturing processes and reducing energy bills through energy efficiency programmes all need to be seen as part of a long-term business ethos not a short-term gimmick.

When a budget is being set, it is not the cost of everything that has to be known, but the priorities. To have every item of expenditure 'fully costed' is unrealistic. It is simply a case of working through a list of needs in order of importance, as finances allow.

Overall, a nation should never be judged by the strength of its economy, but by the way it treats its poor, sick, elderly and vulnerable.

★   Maintain a balanced budget and ensure that all budgetary planning is transparent, presented responsibly and independently audited.

'A strong economy is the foundation for everything we do. It provides higher living standards so that people can look to the future with optimism. It creates the jobs we all depend on - enabling families to build their financial independence. It should guarantee our pensions in old age. It provides a safety net for the least fortunate. It is essential in tackling poverty, including child poverty. It pays for our public services-our children's education and our parents' healthcare. And it allows us to invest in our nation's security -defence, the police and border controls.

Our economic success over generations has been built on the hard work, enterprise and creativity of the British people.

… If we are to secure our future prosperity, government must once again start to live within its means.'
(Conservative Party Election Manifesto 2005, p.3)

'We will give the National Audit Office the power to scrutinize the budget figures, including public borrowing, so that no Chancellor can fiddle the figures.'
(Liberal Democrat Election Manifesto 2005, p. 10-11)

★   Ensure the development of a sustainable economy by initiating closer liaison between government, industry and commerce, but focus mainly on raising the level of exports, by promoting growth in the manufacturing sector/creative industries and encouraging all businesses to consider selling their products abroad. Reform the business rates system in favour of the small/medium sized business sector.

> *'Many small businesses pay a disproportionate amount in rates...We will help small businesses by reforming the business rates system ...'* (Liberal Democrat Election Manifesto 2005, p.10–11)

★ Payment of Income Tax to begin at £12,000 a year for a single person.

> *'What will we do?*
> *... take low-paid workers out of the tax trap by raising the Income Tax threshold for a single person to £12,000 a year.'* (Veritas Election Manifesto 2005, Tax)

> *'Plaid Cymru believes that raising the level at which tax is levied is better and easier for poorer families than a system of complicated credits.'* (Plaid Cymru Election Manifesto 2005, p.4)

Income tax rate of 45% for those earning over £130,000 a year.
All other tax bands to remain the same.

> *'... in God's economy, if a gift is given with the right attitude, the giver benefits even more than the receiver.'*
> (Keith Tondeur)

★ National Insurance rates for those earning £0–£50,000 to remain as at present. Inheritance is a privilege not a right and a tax on assets is a means of the fortunate being able to share their abundance. Inheritance tax payable on property over the value of £200,000, unless the inheritor resides in the property for a minimum of 10 years. Bank of England to remain independent, although when setting the base rate to treat borrowers and savers with equity, retain responsibility for checking inflation, regulate the banking system and monitor the lending and service provision of all banks and building societies. Abolish the Financial Services Authority.

We will maintain the independence of the Bank of England in setting interest rates.'
(Conservative Election Party Manifesto 2005, p. 5)

★   All banks to retain a high level of capital and liquidity. Separate commercial (high street) banking from investment banking.

The Government does not have a responsibility to 'bail out' private companies and any assistance should only be given after very careful consideration. State funding ('bail out') to private companies should only be offered as a loan secured against the company's assets with an agreement that the company will pay back the loan as soon as possible by taking all necessary cost cutting measures and restructuring the business to return it to profitability. Those banks/companies in which the Government does have a share, to allow suitable candidates, i.e. trade union representatives with suitable knowledge and experience, to uphold the public interest, by taking a seat or seats on the board of directors.

Encourage, in the private sector, bonus payment only on the basis of long-term performance Actively pursue tax evasion in the UK and, in cooperation with other countries, seek to regulate large hedge funds and credit rating agencies and close 'tax havens.'

Encourage long-term investment by industry and commerce in companies that seek to promote conservation, are concerned about the environment and the living standards of workers in developing countries. Encourage ethical investment and fair free trade.

'We will work to break down the trade barriers that prevent the poorest countries in the world selling their goods to the richer countries on fair terms.'
(Liberal Democrat Election Manifesto 2005, p.10–11)

★   Encourage personal saving. Minimum age for holding a Debit Card 18 years and a Credit Card 20 years.

★   Encourage charitable giving whilst more closely defining the criteria for charitable status.

'The ProLife Alliance is committed to:

Withdrawing funding and charitable status from agencies which promote anti-life and anti-family values or policies.'
(ProLife Alliance Election Manifesto 2005, p.2)

★   Abolish VAT.

'VAT is administratively over-complex (and therefore expensive to implement) and puts a disproportionate burden on small and medium sized businesses, who act as unpaid tax collectors.'
(Green Party Election Manifesto 2005, p.6)

★   All new mortgages to be based on 2.5 times an individual's income with a minimum 20% deposit. All lenders to work closely with any mortgagees who fall behind with their payments and, in order to seek a resolution of the problem, allow twelve months 'grace' with reduced monthly mortgage payments before repossession proceedings are initiated.

★   Encourage the development of Credit Unions, limit personal borrowing, curb misleading advertising and anti-competitive practices by promoters of insurance for mortgages and loans and credit cards.

★   Lending via banks/financial institutions to be based on relationship and a knowledge of the borrowers total indebtedness. Improve the level of counselling available against getting into debt and assistance to get out of debt. Institute stricter controls on 'fringe' lenders and ensure that mainstream lenders do not pursue 'high risk' lending policies, particularly towards those under 25 years.

'We will tackle irresponsible credit expansion in mortgages and personal loans by curbing misleading advertising and anti-competitive practices by promoters of insurance for mortgages and loans, and of credit cards.'
(Liberal Democrat Election Manifesto 2005, p.10-11)

'The New Party proposes practical policies not only to limit reckless borrowing but also assist those who have got into financial trouble. Stricter

controls on lending especially on the under-25s. Make lenders responsible for establishing a client's total indebtedness in determining whether a loan can be granted.'
(The New Party Election Manifesto 2005, Household Debt)

★   Institute financial support for married couples via Married Couples Allowance and Transferable Tax Allowances so as to encourage one parent to stay at home whilst raising young children. Parents who stay at home to raise their child/children to receive credit toward their National Insurance contributions. End financial assistance toward institutional childcare costs. Abolish the Child Trust Fund.

'Our financial programme backing marriage will not be available to co-habiting couples and is deliberately intended as government recognition of the social responsibilities assumed by two people when they choose to marry. The CPA will introduce Transferable Personal Allowances for Income Tax. This would allow the working spouse to take over the tax-free income allowance of the other spouse. The CPA will reverse the value-neutral attitude of the state towards marriage by re-introducing the Married Couples Allowance.'
(Christian Peoples Alliance Election Manifesto 2005, p.3)

★   Increase maternity grants and child benefit. Child Benefit 0–15 years. Tax Allowances for children 16–18 years.

'TheProLife Alliance is committed to:
Increasing maternity grants and child benefit, and tax allowances for married couples regardless of whether one spouse or both go out to work.'
(ProLife Alliance Election Manifesto 2005, p.2)

★   It is clear that Private Finance Initiatives, because of the substantial cost of the long-term repayments, do not offer the taxpayer value for money. All PFI contracts to be cancelled with the cost of schemes being met through public sector finance.

'The SSP stands for: An end to all PFI schemes …'
(Scottish Socialist Party Election Manifesto 2005, p.28)

'... the current PFI (Public Finance Initiative) is a wasteful and unreliable form of borrowing, which we would phase out.'
Plaid Cymru Election Manifesto 2005, p.4)

'Continue to oppose the use of Public/Private Partnerships and Private Finance Initiatives within health and social services.'
(Sinn Fein Executive Summary 2005, p.5)

★   Allocation to Unitary District Councils of money from UK taxation to be based on assessed need.

'We want to see a broad-based independent commission set up ... to ... review and make detailed recommendations for a needs-based formula for the allocation of public money.'
(Plaid Cymru Election Manifesto 2005, p.5)

★   Until there is surplus money available, limit research connected to space exploration. Discourage the sale of British companies to overseas buyers.

Work, Employment And Benefits

Most people wish to be employed in a fulfilling way and earn their own living thereby avoiding the stigma and/or depression and waste of potential that unemployment brings.

It is important then to bring together those able to be employed and the work that needs to be done. Those who have adopted unemployment as a lifestyle and consider others should keep them in a manner to which they have become accustomed, need to be assisted back into employment as soon as possible, either through retraining or accepting a job they would have previously rejected.

Employment is different from work; you can be unemployed but still work, for example in the voluntary sector. All work, therefore, whether paid or unpaid is of value and help needs to be given to those with available spare time to use it creatively to the benefit of themselves, their families and their neighbourhood.

It is important that workers are not exploited but, equally, a worker has a right to work long hours, provided they are happy to do so, and provided this does not increase a risk to their health and safety or the health and safety of others. Share ownership, where employee's have a share in their employer's business, can be beneficial, as it is then in the employee's long-term interest to see the company achieving good results. The motivation is thus always present for the employee to achieve the highest standards in all they do.

The benefits system needs to be fundamentally reviewed so that it is as straightforward as possible to avoid fraud and also to ensure maximum take up. Those who are eligible for benefits should receive what they are entitled to, rather than endure the demeaning rigours of means testing. As stress and related psychological illnesses in the workplace are a major cause of staff absenteeism and a high cost to the benefits system, employers need to ensure their work practices are humane.

Age does not define us as people, but rather advises and informs us. Employment opportunities therefore need to remain open to anyone who can fulfil the physical or academic requirements.

★Encourage part-time employment at all levels and in all occupations, the right to request flexible working hours for all parents with children under 18, job sharing, and career break schemes to allow parents the opportunity to raise a family. Introduce 18 months of interchangeable parental leave. Encourage married couples and single parents to undertake the care of their children by acknowledging the value of parenting and community involvement.

Ensure equal pay/rights legislation is enforced.

'We support stronger enforcement of equal pay legislation and employment rights protecting the position of part-timers.'
(Plaid Cymru Election Manifesto *2005,* p.8)

★ Employers to encourage a maximum 48 hour week and to ensure employees are not obliged to work longer than they wish, whilst allowing those who desire to work longer to do so, provided this does not increase a risk to their health and safety or the health and safety of others.

'The social costs of long hours are incalculable. People working long hours

MAURICE JONES

are more likely to suffer physical and mental illness and family breakdown.'
(Scottish Socialist Party Election Manifesto 2005, p.14)

★ Reform current Sunday trading legislation to allow only shops of 3000 square feet and under and certain classes of shops/other facilities to open on Sundays. Unitary District Councils to register shops/other facilities based on four criteria:
1) Recreation,
2) Emergencies,
3) Social Gatherings,
4) Traveling Public.

For example:

Petrol stations; Cafes/Restaurants/Takeaway outlets; Sports Centres/ Sporting venues; Cinema's/ Museums/ Historic Houses; Small general food shops/ Chemists, Confectioners/ Newsagents.

★ Provide parents of children under the age of 18 with the right in law to a weekend day off every week. Obligate employers to promote pre-unemployment and post-retirement counselling and pension advice from the outset of employment and to provide sufficient time off for that counselling. Discourage the use of short-term contracts and the unnecessary redeployment of staff. Encourage all employers to institute a 'relational health audit'. Institute individual assessment and specific retraining, or government funded full-time community service placements for all those unemployed for longer than six months and claiming Job Seekers Allowance/Incapacity Benefit, unless their physical/mental disabilities make it genuinely impossible for them to work.

'Liberal Democrats will ... tailor the assistance so that jobseekers receive the package of support they need to get proper, permanent work.'
(Liberal Democrat Election Manifesto 2005, p.12-13)

★ Ensure equal job opportunity based on ability, but allow faith-based employers to uphold their ethos. Encourage innovation and enterprise at all levels of business, but particularly amongst the self-employed.

Encourage share ownership by workers in the companies for whom they work. Encourage opportunities for men and women who wish to continue working after the state retirement age and make it illegal for employers to compel employees to retire at 65.

> 'Forcing older people to prematurely leave their employment robs the economy of decades of knowledge and expertise. We recommend re-training of the older workforce, and we will provide positive solutions to employers, to employ older workforces.'
> (Alliance Party of Northern Ireland Election Manifesto 2005, p.20)

* Restore the link between the Basic State Pension and average earnings with immediate affect. Plan to introduce a State Pension with payment on a 'sliding scale' to men and women from the age of 65 with the full pension being paid from 68 years. 'Ring fence' company pension schemes so neither employers, shareholders or the government can have access to the funds. Consider introducing a Citizens Pension based on residency rather than contributions.

> 'We believe pensioners should receive a substantial increase in the basic state pension. There is no excuse for such high levels of pensioner poverty. The pension system is complicated and individuals need reliable information to help make the right choices. We need a simpler system built on a higher Basic State Pension.'
> (Ulster Democratic Unionist Party Election Manifesto 2005, p.26)

> 'From the age of 75 we will give pensioners our increased 'Citizen's Pension' as of right, making sure that 2.8 million women pensioners have security and dignity in retirement.'
> (Liberal Democrat Election Manifesto 2005, p.12-13)

* Rigorously enforce the responsibility of parents to financially support their children by enhancing and developing the role of the Child Maintenance and Enforcement Commission. Parents who fail to pay child maintenance to have the money taken directly from their wages or via the courts by, where necessary:

★ seizing non-resident parents' belongings and selling them;

★ freezing money belonging to, or owed to them;

★ registering their debt so that it effects the transfer or sale of property or assets;

★ forcing the sale of property owned by the non-resident parent.

The courts also to have the power to confiscate their driving license or stop them from obtaining one for three years.

★ Review the Benefits System with the aim of simplifying the process of claiming and eliminating benefit fraud and error. Consider changing from paying out benefits, to increasing personal tax allowances. Benefits based upon entitlement rather than means tested. Substantially improve the allowances paid to those caring for an ill, frail or disabled person in the community. Offer advice and training on budgeting.

> 'We support moving away from means testing in order to ensure all pensioners receive a decent income.' (Ulster Democratic Unionist Party Election Manifesto 2005, p.26)

★ Substantially raise the minimum statutory hourly rate for workers aged 22 and over.

> 'Low pay goes hand in hand with long hours and poor conditions.
>
> Low paid workers are less likely to be members of occupational pension schemes, creating a lifetime of poverty.' (Scottish Socialist Party Election Manifesto 2005, P.14)

Trade Unions

Although trade unions have, for many years, helped to improve the conditions of workers, they sometimes now impede, rather than encourage good industrial relations.

Employers have a responsibility to treat their employees justly, as a manager's first priority in whatever sphere is always to promote the interests of those in their charge and lead them by example. Likewise, employees have a responsibility to respect the decisions of their employers.

In order to speak without bias for all their members and remain focussed on their core objective, i.e. employee/employer relations, trade unions need to become neutral in their affiliations.

Trade unions need to be progressively remodelled into a form that removes the distinctions and barriers between employees and management thus eliminating the need for strike action by ensuring continual dialogue. For dialogue is never a sign of weakness, and strikes, like wars, often destroy more than they achieve.

★   All companies employing over 400 people to have one or more union representatives on their main management boards and increased employee representation at all levels of management.

★   Ban trade union political affiliation and end all financial donations to political parties.

Health And Social Care

The Government has a responsibility to invest in the health and care of all its citizens, whatever their age, by generously funding from taxation a high quality, integrated, well-defined national health and social care service that is equally available to everyone, free at the point of use and locally accountable, the overriding principle being for people to pay according to their means and to receive according to their need.

Healthcare is about more than treating the greatest number of people at the lowest possible cost. A caring national health service should not only seek to treat each person as an individual of equal worth, but also offer the same level of care and facilities as the private sector.

Although the rapid advances in medical treatment are to be welcomed and honest research rewarded, 'speculative' medical research that uses unethical means to achieve its results and unfairly raises the expectations of patients should be discouraged. The Health Service needs to give a high priority to the prevention of illness through the promotion of healthy eating/healthy living/physical exercise and the dangers of a sedentary lifestyle. However, although obesity particularly is a time bomb, as people cannot be forced to change their lifestyles, without personal motivation helpful initiatives and the time of medical staff are wasted. Unless therefore there is demonstrable evidence by the individual (child or adult) concerned to change their behaviour, incentives need to be restricted and responsibility placed on the individual to manage their life without demanding special treatment.

The Health Service also has a role in bringing about a seed change in attitudes regarding the sexualisation of children, teenagers and young adults by assisting parents, perhaps through parenting courses, to regain the confidence to set boundaries for them, to help young males regain a respect for female bodies and for young females to regain the courage to say 'no', so that not only are unwanted pregnancies avoided, but also the negative emotional and physical consequences of abortion and early teenage parenthood.

Janice Turner writing in the *THE TIMES* in March 2009 comments,

> 'Girls are programmed to please; more vulnerable than boys to the opinions of others; more eager to fulfil prevailing expectations. When being brainy was deemed unfeminine, they underachieved; now that getting 10A*s is cool, they excel. When being drunk was unladylike, they stayed on their feet. It is not a hitherto repressed thirst for liquor that makes teenage girls now three times more likely than boys to be treated for alcoholic poisoning, but the fashionable notion that they should love to party.'

Turner continues,

> 'A women's glossy magazine rang me this week about a survey showing that female twentysomethings now seek out one-night stands as readily as any man. Wasn't this, I was asked, magnificently empowered? Only, I had to demur, if it's what they really really want. Are the American high school girls taking part in oral-sex contests, girls who send snaps of their breast to be assessed on lads-mags websites, the 15-year-old girls having unprotected sex also empowered? Isn't it just too much of a coincidence that these images of supposed liberated female sexuality just happen to

mirror male fantasies. Shame, fear and a horror of being thought a slag
used to stop girls having sex. They weren't great excuses and often little
impediment. But they were flags to wave when girls really meant "I'm not
ready". Now even "I don't want to" isn't enough when fashion dictates
that a girl must appear to want to, all the time.

If only we could truly empower girls, help them to distinguish between
desire and coercion, show them how – without losing face – it is possible
to say no.'

Monitoring of health service provision should be the responsibility of
Unitary District Councils pursuing nationally agreed goals and
standards that seek to progress the quality of patient care.

Co-ordinated community care, i.e. enabling the elderly, dying, sick
or disabled to enjoy an enhanced quality of life in their own homes for
as long as possible, should also be a priority, along with helping to
change attitudes towards those with learning difficulties, physical
incapacity or mental illness, by concentrating on people's abilities, rather
than their disabilities and, for those who are impaired, to view their
impairment not as a burden but as a part of who they are, something
to work with and use positively, thereby enabling them to direct their
own lives, achieve their own goals and live the life they choose.

Although life expectancy is increasing, even with medical advances
an individual's quality of health in old age is not guaranteed. Substantial
investment is therefore required in the field of social care to enable
elderly people to enjoy their final years as independently and as pain
free as possible.

Providing good quality healthcare requires a high level of
emotional investment.

If patients are to be treated as human beings not statistics, the
emphasis needs to be on the promotion of human relationships within
hospitals/surgeries. For patients to be viewed 'holistically', as often the
emotional, mental, relational, spiritual and physical aspects of peoples
lives are inter-related. Healthcare facilities therefore need to be run not
as businesses but as communities, with practitioners being encouraged
to build relationships with those for whom they have responsibility.

Life is precious. From the moment when a sperm fuses with an
ovum and the potential for human life begins, to a person's last breath,

the emphasis of the NHS must be the care of, and respect for, every individual.

'Good quality public services, freely available to all, are key to the development of a more equitable and secure society. Increasingly, however, we are seeing health, education and other services come under pressure to adopt the principles and practices of the market place, with growing levels of privatisation and private sector delivery. Such commercialisation is undermining the universality and, particularly in the case of the NHS, the comprehensiveness, that used to be a hallmark of the UK's welfare state.

Prevention is better than cure. A great deal of our national health spending is wasted on treating the cocktail of social and poverty-driven illnesses caused by factors such as air pollution, overwork, junk food and poor quality housing. A Green government will develop health services that place as much emphasis on illness prevention, health promotion and the development of individual and community self-reliance as on the treatment and cure of disease. We will particularly tackle the growing and preventable mental health crisis being triggered by our over-competitive and market-driven culture.

The Green Party rejects the nostrum of patient choice, which actually undermines the NHS by replicating services, often using private providers, in order to offer the illusion of choice. We do not support the creation of a two-tier NHS caused by the introduction of foundation hospitals.'
(Green Party Election Manifesto 2005, p.14)

'A compassionate society that values relationships above material possessions will be a slower and less dysfunctional society. How does this make Christian Democratic health policy different? The CPA aims to restore healing and health to its rightful place in policy making. So, health problems associated with the consumerist society will be made part of the economic equation and not just addressed once people become ill.
This means watching out for the stress that modern life in Britain loads on people, especially the less well off who are most likely to suffer health problems. Employers will be asked to address working hours, especially weekend working, so that time is released for people to spend in rest and recreation and in developing relationships, especially with older relatives and children. An economy less demanding of energy will see a reduction in

pollution. Less reliance on industrialised food production will also have direct health benefits.'
(Christian Peoples Alliance Election Manifesto 2005, p.5)

'We believe it is important that older people are not discriminated against on the grounds of age, but are able to participate fully in society and their local community. Doctors admit to denying patients access to medical treatment from their early 60s ... The DUP supports legislation to prevent discrimination against older people in society.'
(Ulster Democratic Unionist Party Election Manifesto 2005, p.27)

★   Institute a common National Health Care System.

★   Unitary District Councils to be responsible for monitoring all hospitals and other healthcare services in their locality and liaising with the County Planning Group regarding local needs.

★   Abolish all Primary Care Trusts and end the purchaser/provider split within the NHS. End the system of foundation hospitals.

★   Overall hospital management to rest with the hospital manager and senior medical staff, assisted equally by a representative from the Unitary District Council and patient/community representatives. Limit the areas of budgetary responsibility for hospitals and GPs.

★   Replace 'polyclinics' with the development of urban community health centres which are open during the day and early evening and which promote community health programmes, health education, screening, counselling/citizens advice and are the base for local GPs, district nurses and community social workers.
     Enable GPs to undertake a higher number of minor operations, tests and scans to ensure early diagnosis and treatment.

'More tests and scans will be available in places like GPs' surgeries ...'
(Liberal Democrat Election Manifesto 2005, p. 04–05)

All rural surgeries to dispense medicines. All surgeries to open Saturday mornings.

Ensure a comprehensive 'out of hours' service managed and staffed by local GPs. General health examinations to be offered by GPs to adults in their places of employment.

Enhance the services of NHS Direct.

Encourage the growth and development of GP managed, local community hospitals that incoporate minor A and E units, provide a wide range of day care surgery, outpatients and diagnostic tests, alongside rehabilitation and community nursing.

Specialist services to be offered in district hospitals with increased local outpatient clinics. Localize ambulance services.

★   Ensure that all healthcare buildings are maintained to a high level.

★   Waiting lists to be progressively reduced and permanently removed by an increase in staffing levels, the opening of closed wards and substantial investment in discharge/rehabilitation services.

'What will we do?

Reduce waiting-lists by allocating more resources to the NHS.'
(Veritas Election Manifesto 2005, Health)

'Steps to be taken to make it easier for people to move out of hospital when their treatment is completed or when hospital is not the best place for them.'
(Plaid Cymru Election Manifesto 2005, p.10)

★   Encourage the growth and development of in-service training courses for all levels of nursing staff, based on holistic care. Promote confidential bi-annual in-house appraisal of all nursing staff focussed on career and professional development. Promote schemes that encourage staff retention, and those who have left the profession to return. Ensure anonymity for NHS staff who are the subject of malicious and unfounded allegations of misconduct.

★   Abolish hospital car parking fees.

★   Agree national standards for all hospitals. End 'league tables' and remove unnecessary bureaucracy.

'The CPA will restore fair access to health care by ensuring that national standards of provision are the bench marks…'
(Christian Peoples Alliance Election Manifesto 2005, p.5)

'What will we do?

drastically reduce health service bureaucracy by … abolishing meaningless league tables and unnecessary statistics keeping.'
(Veritas Election Manifesto 2005, Health)

★   All hospital cleaning services to be 'in-house' and under the responsibility of senior nursing staff.

★   Establish a National Health Service Inspectorate employed by the Department of Health. All hospitals, GP surgeries and other health establishments (including all private health facilities) to receive random spot checks.

★   NHS to fund only evidence-based complimentary medicine/therapies. Medication recommended by N.I.C.E. to be available to all patients as required. but encourage GPs to use other means of treatment, rather than drug therapy, when appropriate. Encourage GPs to avoid the 'medicalisation' of bad behaviour in children that could be more effectively dealt with in other ways and, also, behaviour that does not fit a prescribed pattern, so as to avoid restricting the child's development and the onset of neurosis in the parents.

★   Extend research into pain relief for those who are terminally ill and further develop the role of pain relief clinics. Substantially expand the role of Macmillan nurses and adequately fund the provision of local hospices. Also, expand the Hospice at Home service so that end-of-life patients can receive 24 hour practical and emotional support in their own homes for as long as possible.

'What will we do?

provide adequate funding to the hospice movement.'
(Veritas Election Manifesto 2005, Health)

'The ProLife Alliance is committed to:
hospices (capital and running costs) which provide terminal or palliative
and respite care for adults, children and infants.'
(ProLife Alliance Election Manifesto 2005, p. 2)

'The CPA will develop ways of promoting the hospice movement ...'
(Christian Peoples Alliance Election Manifesto 2005, p. 5)

Allow the elderly to die with dignity, by not prolonging invasive medicine. Oppose euthanasia in all its forms as there is a world of difference between people choosing to stop their medication or treatment and dying naturally and choosing to be injected with poison in order to terminate their life. Those assisting a suicide whether in the UK or abroad to face a jail sentence of up to 10 years.

'It is never justified to treat older people as less entitled to life and respect
merely because of their age or because of frailty. Deliberate acts leading to
the death of older people by healthcare professionals will be exposed and
policies to introduce euthanasia by the back door will be rooted out. Best
practice in palliative care will be adopted nationally across all health and
social care authorities so that no patient need seek either assisted suicide
or euthanasia.'
(Christian Peoples Alliance Election Manifesto 2005, p.5)

'The ProLife Alliance will:
outlaw voluntary, non-voluntary and involuntary euthanasia by omission
or by direct act, including neonatal euthanasia and euthanasia of patients
in a 'persistent vegetative state'.
(ProLife Alliance Election Manifesto 2005, p.2)

★   Promote regular free eye and teeth check-ups for all ages. Review and revise NHS dental contracts to ensure there are an acceptable number of dentists willing to undertake NHS work. Provide free digital hearing aids for those who need them.

'To reduce the risk of illness going undetected we will end the charges for eye
and dental check-ups which deter people from coming forward for testing.'
(Liberal Democrat Election Manifesto 2005, p.04–05)

'Many people can't find an NHS dentist to take them on. We will reform NHS dental contracts so that more dentists are encouraged to do more NHS work.'
(Liberal Democrat Election Manifesto 2005, p.04–05)

'We will introduce free eye tests and dental checks.'
(Plaid Cymru Election Manifesto 2005, p.10)

'Abolish eye and dental check charges, and ensure the availability of NHS dental care.
Provide free digital hearing aids for those who need them.'
(Alliance Party of Northern Ireland Election Manifesto 2005, p.15)

★ Promote the development of foetal surgery and medicine – correcting malformations and conditions in unborn babies that would otherwise result in severe health problems or death. Provide comprehensive ante-natal healthcare for women who choose to have their baby delivered at home. Substantially increase the numbers of midwives and health visitors to monitor the growth and development of babies/young children and offer advice/support where necessary. Encourage breast feeding where possible, as breast fed babies are rarely obese.

★ Expand re-enablement services that provide intensive short-term support to assist people following an operation or illness to regain their confidence, their independence, and lost skills, and take control of their lives. Ensure the close monitoring of all patient discharges into the community. Personalise cancer care during and after treatment.

★ Develop primary and community care-based mental health services, including out-of-hours support to assist all those diagnosed with a mental health problem, particularly a severe mental illness i.e. schizophrenia or severe depression. Develop screening services to assist in the early diagnoses of illnesses such as dementia.

'Develop primary and community care-based mental health services, including out-of-hours services. This can ensure early, skilled intervention, as well as to prevent admissions to hospital.'
(Alliance Party of Northern Ireland Election Manifesto 2005, p.16)

★ Assist hospitals, GPs and other agencies to become integral parts of a coordinated health and social care system.

Field and hospital Social Workers to be experienced, well supported/supervised highly trained specialists in the assessment of need, counselling, establishing and developing productive relationships, understanding the complexities of their particular client group and allowing clients the autonomy, as far as is possible to have a controlling say in how their needs are met.

Ensure early and comprehensive intervention for vulnerable children living in dysfunctional homes. Social Workers involved in child protection to base their investigations and actions on a) a realistic scepticism of family relationships, b) the fact that the child is their client and therefore the child's welfare is always paramount, c) regular visits to the child, close liaison with other professionals and physically examining the child when necessary and d) regular supervision with manager's who are willing to make difficult decisions and who ensure any fail-safe mechanisms are strictly adhered too.

★ Expand the use of Unitary District Council Home-Carers to assist those who live alone and require care, or to relieve caring relatives and substantially increase the availability of respite care. Personal care at home to be based on need and be free of charge. Increase the recognition of and financial support for carers who look after the welfare of their sick and dependent relatives.

'The SSP stands for: Increased support for carers.'
(Scottish Socialist Party Election Manifesto 2005, p.33)

'Carers who look after elderly people or disabled relatives, including those suffering from long-term conditions, deserve more support. We will boost respite for carers and give them more choice and information about the support available.'
(Conservative Party Election Manifesto 2005, p.12)

'Increased support for carers looking after people in their own homes, so that they do not reach a point where putting someone in hospital comes to look like the only practical option.'
(Plaid Cymru Election Manifesto 2005, p.10)

> *'Provide recognition and financial support to carers, who look after the welfare of their sick and dependent relatives. Establish a respite care system that is flexible, reliable and meets the need of carers and those they care for.'*
> (Alliance Party of Northern Ireland Election Manifesto 2005, p.23)

Encourage the development of 'extra-care' warden supervised accommodation/supported living as an alternative to traditional residential homes. Encourage the development of 'homeshare' schemes, where householders in need of company and help around the home are paired with able-bodied people in return for rent-free or cheap accommodation.

Home adaptations and equipment to be provided to enable the elderly and terminally ill to live independently in their own homes for as long as possible.

Develop 'adopt a granny/granddad' schemes. Encourage the development of 'homeshare daycare' schemes, where a person opens their home to offer daycare to one or more elderly people and also ensure the adequate provision of local daycare centres.

The cost of long-term care to be free in local authority residential/nursing homes. Those choosing to be admitted into private residential/nursing homes to pay the full cost of their care.

Admission to local authority residential or nursing care to be based on absolute medical or social necessity.

> *'Introduce free personal care for those living in residential and nursing homes.'*
> (Alliance Party of Northern Ireland Election Manifesto 2005, p.15)

> *'The DUP is committed to the introduction of free personal care as well as free nursing care for the elderly.'*
> (Ulster Democratic Unionist Party Election Manifesto 2005, p.26)

> *'Those towards the end of their lives deserve the best possible care. Liberal Democrats will provide free personal care for elderly people and people with disabilities, for as long as they need it ...'*
> (Liberal Democrat Election Manifesto 2005, p.04–05)

★   Substantially increase the number of residential/nursing homes owned and managed by Unitary District Councils with all placements being arranged via Social Services. Care in residential/nursing homes to be based on individual social, emotional and physical needs.

All residential/nursing homes to be subject to regular vigorous inspection. All agencies who work with vulnerable adults to log and investigate reports of abuse, either in residential/nursing care or in family homes, and ensure that their findings are passed to the appropriate authority for further investigation and action.

* Repeal the 1967 Abortion Act. Restrict the need for abortion except where, because of severe medical complications, the life of the child threatens the life of the mother. Provide comprehensive birth control advice and counselling for young people and those who have had or who are considering an abortion. End the screening out of abnormalities in embryos. All mothers to be required to name the father of their baby on birth certificates.

'The right to life is the right from which all others flow... we will seek to repeal the 1967 Abortion Act. An end will be put to the use of the morning after pill.

The screening out of abnormalities in embryos will be ended and a commitment made to listening and acting on the needs, views and interests of people with disabilities or long-term illness. Additionally, in conjunction with local authorities, caring agencies and the faith communities, the CPA will ensure that no woman seeks an abortion because of lack of accommodation, baby essentials, cots, prams or clothes. A public health campaign will be run warning of the consequences of abortion, such as post-abortion syndrome, health complications and the associated risks of breast cancer. The CPA will ensure the provision of a 24-hour, 7-day a week helpline for women and couples considering abortion.'
(Christian Peoples Alliance Election Manifesto 2005, p.5)

'The ProLife Alliance will:
repeal the Abortion Act 1967 and outlaw all abortion, except when the baby's death is brought about indirectly, for example, as a side-effect of medical treatment for the mother.

The ProLife Alliance is committed to:
pro-life pregnancy care services, including provision of accommodation for
women made homeless by pregnancy, pregnant women with special needs
and one-parent families, and post-abortion counselling.'
(ProLife Alliance Election Manifesto 2005, p.2)

★ Encourage a worldwide ban on surrogacy. All children already born to surrogate mothers and those conceived from donated sperm, to be allowed to trace their biological parent.

★ Puberty is a difficult time for any young person as their bodies change physically and their hormones make them feel new and unusual things. Sexuality and identity are part of those changes. Although homophobia i.e. the irrational fear or hatred of homosexuals should always be renounced, because of the vulnerability of children and teenagers during this time, the minimum age of consent for homosexuals/lesbians to be 22 years.

★ Expand fostering services and ensure adequate support and training for foster carers. Develop a wide range of fostering options such as: *Short-term* (caring for children for a few weeks or months until difficulties at home are resolved or alternative plans made for the child's future); *Short breaks (Respite)*, (offering a resource to struggling families or to other foster carers needing a break themselves); *Remand* (offering care and support in collaboration with the Youth Offending Services, for young people who have been remanded by the courts and are awaiting their next hearing); *Mother and baby* (supporting young mothers who need additional guidance to care for their babies safely); *Emergency* (caring for a child/children at very short notice because of a family crisis); and *Long-term/Permanent* (caring for a baby/child/young person as they grow up and until they are ready to live independently). Fostering and adoption to be undertaken only by married, heterosexual couples over 25 and able to provide a caring, stable home. Upper age to adopt, 40 years without exception. Discourage the adoption of foreign children.

★ Provide a high level of rehabilitation for drug and alcohol abusers, whilst seeking to educate children/teenagers through contemporary means, i.e. dance, drama, music and art against the use of drugs. Tackle the root causes of each addiction whilst adopting a 'zero tolerance' approach towards those who financially benefit from the illegal import, distribution and sale of drugs, alcohol and cigarettes. Encourage the growing of drugs abroad for medical use.

Maintain the classification of drugs as laid out in the Misuse of Drugs Act 1971 with cannabis being classified as a Class B drug.

'Drugs remain a significant danger for our young people...We will continue to press for greater resources to tackle this problem, and better education to prevent more of our young people being drawn into this dangerous world.'
(Ulster Democratic Unionist Party Election Manifesto 2005, p.19)

'The SSP stands for:
The establishment of a network of community-based rehabilitation services staffed by trained drug workers.'
(Scottish Socialist Party Election Manifesto 2005, p. 45)

'More drug rehabilitation places and programmes, partly funded from confiscated drugs money,'
(Plaid Cymru Election Manifesto 2005, p. 13)

★ As availability and cheapness are two of the main contributors to binge drinking and alcohol related illness, restrict pub closing times to 11pm. Restrict club closing times to 2am. Encourage the opening of non-alcoholic pubs and clubs for those aged 14 plus and encourage the development of alternative amenities. End the sale of alcoholic drinks apart from table wines, from all retail food outlets. Alcoholic drinks to be purchased only from restaurants, public houses, clubs, off-licenses, hotels/guest houses. Taxation on alcoholic drinks to be based on alcohol content. Ban cheap alcohol promotions and pursue any effective strategy that discourages high levels of alcohol consumption. Minimum age for purchasing alcohol 22 years.

Alcohol advertising to be limited and alcohol sponsorship to be banned, where possible, in the UK. Shops, restaurants, public houses, clubs, off-licenses, hotels/guest houses to be regularly inspected to ensure they are fulfilling their legal obligations.

'The SSP stands for: An all-out education and propaganda offensive against Scotland's binge-drinking culture.'
(Scottish Socialist Party Election Manifesto 2005, p.45)

'Better amenities for young people in their communities to help counter the attractions of town centre binge drinking.
Stricter controls on how drinks are advertised and marketed, including health warnings.'
(Plaid Cymru Election Manifesto 2005, p.13)

★ Minimum age for purchasing cigarettes 22 years. Raise the tax on cigarettes by 25% and end their sale from all food outlets. Vigorously promote the benefits of exercise and ensure the promotion of healthy eating within schools and homes. Ban the advertising of unhealthy food and drink during children's television programs. Ensure the limiting of food additives in all food. Ensure the very highest food and hygiene standards in all food outlets by regular, rigorous inspection and an upward revision of penalties.

'Individuals should be encouraged to adopt greater personal responsibility for healthy living, particularly in relation to diet and exercise, binge drinking, smoking and illicit drug use.'
(Ulster Democratic Unionist Party Election Manifesto 2005, p.21)

'We … would support an increase in the price of cigarettes to pay for front line health services.'
(Alliance Party of Northern Ireland Election Manifesto 2005, p.15)

'If the causes of ill-health aren't tackled, the NHS of the future won't be able to cope - so we will give people the information and opportunities to make healthy choices, for example through clearer food and alcohol labeling. To improve children's health, on top of plans to increase funding for school meals, we will introduce minimum nutrition standards for school meals … we will restrict advertising of unhealthy food during children's television programmes;'
(Liberal Democrat Election Manifesto 2005, p.04–05)

'We need to tackle the causes of ill-health. These include not only long-

*standing causes such as poverty and unhealthy working and housing
conditions, but increasingly also the misuse of drugs, lack of exercise, and
exploitative marketing to young children. Plaid Cymru will seek a ban
on the advertising of unhealthy food and drink on children's television ...'*
(Plaid Cymru Election Manifesto 2005, p.11)

★   Closely monitor and assess advances in medical technology with
regard to their general benefit and application, particularly genetic
engineering.

★   Although infertility requires clinical investigation, parenthood can
be achieved through other means i.e. adoption. In vitro fertilisation
(IVF) treatment should only be offered on the NHS to those married
couples willing to make any necessary adjustment to their lifestyle i.e.
give up smoking or loose weight, in order for the procedure to have a
higher degree of success. Suitable couples to be offered three cycles of
IVF treatment once the woman is 30 years. Because of the low rate of
conception, treatment to be offered only after careful consideration to
women 35-40 years. Uphold the ban on selling sperm and eggs and any
other body parts.

★   Promote research into the use of adult stem cells in providing cures
for serious illnesses. Ban embryonic research/experimentation that
permits the creation of human–animal hybrids. Ban the creation of
saviour siblings, the deliberate creation of children with the intention
they should be denied a father for the duration of their childhood (i.e.
IVF for lesbian couples), the deliberate creation of children with the
intention they should be denied a mother from six months (i.e. male
couples using a surrogate mother), and human reproductive cloning.
Ban, as far as is possible, internet services that provide anonymous
sperm donors for lesbian couples.
   Encourage research into the use of a person's own bone marrow
stem cells to grow replacement organs and the use of gene therapy to
treat those who have inherited defective genes.

*'The ProLife Alliance will ... outlaw cloning, embryo experiments and
all reproductive technologies where more embryos are created than are
immediately transferred to the mother's body.*

The ProLife Alliance is committed to:
pro-life fertility awareness and control, and pro-life infertility treatment
pro-life medical and scientific research, especially into human infertility and
the use of adult stem cells to treat disease.'
(ProLife Alliance Election Manifesto 2005, p.2)

'Cloning of human beings and embryo experimentation will be outlawed.'
(Christian Peoples Alliance Election Manifesto 2005, p.5)

★   Ensure that cybernetics and indeed all technological advances that relate to the 'enhancing' of the human body, are used in good and moral ways under the guiding principle that 'just because we can doesn't mean we should'.

★   Ensure equal rights for those with disabilities and that the necessary services are provided to meet their needs. Promote the positive aspects of disability by focusing on what can be achieved rather than on what has been lost. Promote the education, training and support of young people with physical disabilities or learning difficulties and assist them to experience the realities of real 9-5 jobs.

'We accept the social rather than medical model of disability, and seek improved rehabilitation services and provision of allied health professionals.'
(Ulster Democratic Unionist Party Election Manifesto 2005, p.21)

'Meaningful employment targets, including within the public sector, to address unacceptable levels of unemployment amongst people with disabilities,

All public buildings should conform to universal design standards with regard to accessibility,

Right to advocacy for people with mental disabilities.'
(Sinn Fein Executive Summary 2005, p.7)

'Develop community services for people with learning difficulties. We are particularly concerned at the shortfalls in day and respite care as well as in employment opportunities.
(Alliance Party of Northern Ireland Election Manifesto 2005, p.16)

Improve access to public facilities for all disabled people. This will be achieved through comprehensive access policies.'
(Alliance Party of Northern Ireland Election Manifesto 2005, p.23)

★ No presumed consent for organ donation. Encourage those who wish to donate their organs to make their wishes clear to their family and formally to a central register. Increase the number of surgeons and operating theatres available for organ transplants.

Education And Training

The Government has a responsibility to invest in the future of all its citizens, whatever their age, by generously funding from taxation, a high quality, integrated, national education and training system with local accountability.

Education is about more than teaching the greatest number at the lowest possible cost. A productive education system should not only seek to treat each person as an individual of equal worth, but also offer the same level of opportunities and facilities as the private sector.

Education has a value that cannot be reduced to a balance sheet. Neither is education a means of turning children into exam fodder in preparation for the workplace. For, if the purpose of education is only to produce people capable of contributing to the economy with their brains alone, those who will never be able to contribute academically, or only contribute in a limited way, will inevitably be under-valued. The policy of 'University education for all' is therefore flawed as not only does it lessen the value of the degree itself and saturates the jobs market with 'graduates', it also diverts resources away from encouraging the creative side of children (as every child and indeed adult has a creative spirit within them), to develop. The education system needs, therefore, to offer many more vocational options to young people who are not suited to academic learning and also opportunities to learn in the workplace, whatever that workplace might be, in order to gain skills and experience.

Education should encourage every child to reach their full potential intellectually, to think independently by giving them all the options, to work co-operatively, to enjoy curiosity, to make a positive contribution to their community, to develop a wide range of life skills that will fit the child for adult life and also be concerned for the child's overall well-being. Thus developing a child who is equipped to make the most of their opportunities, fulfil their ambitions and retains a passion for learning.

Information and Communication Technology (ICT) is a useful tool, but it only offers visual, often passive, indoor learning that does not engage the other senses. If computer literate young people cannot verbally communicate, write coherently and inventively, relate to other human beings because their contact with real people has been limited and cannot relate to the world around them because they have enjoyed few real life experiences, they will be condemned to lead an impoverished adult life.

In short then, the education system should assist in the development and nurture of the whole child, body, mind and spirit, thereby fashioning a young person who has a high level of self-confidence, self-respect, adaptability, an ability to retain what they have been taught, a sense of social justice and national citizenship, a respectful outlook towards others, who are aware of the beauty of the world around them, can practice common sense, who can learn from their mistakes, who are innovative and capable of imaginative expression, are able to express their emotions, able to share, lose and fail, take calculated risks, who have a sense of adventure and a balanced view of the world.

Teachers, therefore, have the difficult balancing act of not only helping children discover and cultivate their talents in every area, but also of ensuring all children are literate, numerate and articulate by the time they transfer from primary to secondary school.

Providing good quality education requires a high level of emotional investment. If children are to be treated as human beings not statistics, the emphasis needs to be on the promotion of human relationships within schools/colleges, for children to be viewed 'holistically' as often the emotional, mental, relational, spiritual and physical aspects of children's lives are inter-related. Educational facilities therefore need to be run, not as businesses but as communities, with teachers being encouraged to build relationships with those for whom they have responsibility.

Although children need to be regularly assessed as to their progress throughout their school career, this should not be overly prescriptive, in order to take account of variations in child development. Exam results measure only a small part of what a particular child might be achieving. Their level of attainment therefore should be based mainly on continual teacher assessment, externally moderated as applicable, that gives robust and reliable information to pupils, parents, other teachers and other schools, with school inspectors considering the educational well-being of the whole child and school situation rather than any raw data gleaned from tests.

The aim of education should be to achieve a level of excellence in every pupil based on their distinct abilities rather than mass comparisons and for every pupil to discover that education is of value in itself rather than just as a preparation for employment. Wisdom, and creativity rather than grades should be its objective.

The education system does not primarily exist to ensure every pupil achieves 'A' in every exam but is part of a process to produce a reflective human being. A child with straight A grades isn't necessarily an educated child.

Education of children is a shared responsibility with all adults having an obligation to set an example to those in school or further education. Ultimately, a child who is the product of a supportive society will not only be well educated, but with the joint involvement and partnership of home, school and community and the benefit of a balanced, high quality, flexible curriculum that ensures the attainment of basic literacy and numeracy skills yet is broad enough to engage all concerned, will be assisted to become a well-rounded member of the human race.

Schools should be at the heart of their community and act as a base for children and adults to access other resources and share activities. Monitoring of education provision should be the responsibility of the Unitary District Council, pursuing nationally agreed goals and standards that seek to progress the quality of learning. Poverty is sometimes used as a reason for a child's underachievement at school. It is not the case however that low income automatically leads to poor academic results. When parents take a full interest in their child's schooling and a child experiences dynamic teaching, even children emanating from financially modest backgrounds can become highly successful adults. In recent years there has been a move towards schools taking on the dubious role of surrogate parenting particularly as a means of abolishing poverty through parental employment. This though has undermined parental bonding. In order to build strong, stable family relationships and assist children in their preparation for school and indeed, throughout their school life, children need to spend as much time as possible with their parents. If poverty is an issue, then other means of raising a family's standard of living need to be embraced, rather than separating young children from their parents via institutional childcare. Children were given to be enjoyed by parents, not exiled from them.

Although every child, from every background, whatever their faith should be welcome in any educational establishment and no school should ever proselytize, schools do have a responsibility to give all children a 'moral compass'. To help them develop a sense of right and wrong through an understanding of Judaeo–Christian values. Thus all schools should have a holistic approach to education that includes spiritual and moral well-being. With representatives from other faiths being encouraged into schools to give pupils a rounded view of religion and parents being encouraged to teach their children at home, the deeper aspects of their own particular faith.

Education should be available to any, particularly the elderly who are often 'written off' by society, who in later years may wish to retrain/gain qualifications/learn for pleasure, so as to help people appreciate that education is for life, not just for children.

'The Green Party is committed to life-long education opportunities for all. A fully rounded education - not just skills for the workplace - is necessary to help people to reach their full potential as human beings and is a foundation for an equitable and sustainable society.'
(Green Party Election Manifesto 2005, p.15)

'There has also been a narrowing down in governments' understanding of the purposes of education, so that it is seen as simply about meeting the requirements of employers. Important though these are, education is also about the development of creativity, a well-informed democracy, and an understanding and appreciation of the world around us.

To undermine and demoralise teachers in the way that recent governments have done is to squander an extremely valuable asset. … We value the whole team in our schools, including support staff.'
(Plaid Cymru Election Manifesto 2005, p.11)

'The approach which marks out the Christian Peoples Alliance is our commitment to the highest ideals of liberal education - the formation of the whole person. Schooling at its best opens up new horizons, broadens the imagination, gives space to the flourishing of the human spirit and helps form the character of the individual. For this reason Christian Democrats do not believe that education is primarily about exam results and league tables. Our approach is to impart a clear sense of moral rights and responsibilities and foster good ideas of citizenship. Lack of self-esteem in young people is often paralleled by self-obsessions. These are products of the pressures of our consumerist culture, where to be rich, attractive or powerful are held up as the highest goals of life. Space is needed in schools to allow worldly values to be tested and true self-love to be understood. The CPA will therefore cut back on the requirements of the National Curriculum in order to allow teachers to impart the gifts of their vocation ...

Schools cannot be expected to deal with every problem of society. Education begins first in the home and continues through life. The CPA will not rely on testing in schools and educational re-organisation to improve educational outcomes. Just as important to children and raising standards is tackling poverty and supporting stability in the home, which comes through loving parental relationships. For this reason, schools will be places where honesty, motivation, self-worth, moral values and a respect for God and neighbour are valued as highly as prowess in other areas of school life.'
(Christian Peoples Alliance Election Manifesto 2005, p.4)

'Access to education is vital to ensure that every individual has the opportunity to realise his or her full potential. Alliance supports a universal education system, free at the point of access. Government should adequately cater for the demands of nursery, primary, secondary and tertiary places. Furthermore, Alliance believes in lifelong learning and training. Educational opportunities must be available to all at every stage of life. The system needs to be sufficiently flexible to cater for a range of demands and abilities. The current education system serves well those most academically able, but does not adequately address the needs of pupils across the full spectrum of ability.'
(Alliance Party of Northern Ireland Election Manifesto 2005, p.13)

★ Institute a common National Education System.

★ Pursue the national introduction of the Assessing Pupil Progress (APP) approach to assessment, in all subjects, that equips teachers to make consistent and reliable judgements on pupils' progress.

★ Unitary District Councils to be responsible for monitoring all schools and other educational establishments in their locality and liaising with the County Planning Group regarding local needs.

★ Overall school management, strategic direction, the appointment (but not employment) of staff and general responsibility for all aspects of school life to rest with the head teacher, assisted by a representative from the Unitary District Council and in equal number by parent/community/teacher/local mainstream Christian governors, who are fully committed to the well-being of the school and whose brief is to be 'supportive friends' to the head teacher. Limit the areas of budgetary responsibility in schools, colleges and universities. All teachers to receive a high standard of initial training. Selection based on personality as well as intellectual ability. Encourage the growth and development of in-service training courses for all levels of staff.

★ Ensure regular peer support for head teachers. Ensure teachers have sufficient release time to fulfil their duties. Institute confidential, bi-annual, in-house appraisal of all staff focussed on career and professional development. Promote schemes that encourage staff retention and those who have left the profession to return. Assist parents to understand their role in preparing their child to learn in a collaborative, structured environment and of the benefit of continuing their involvement in their child's education after school hours and during school holidays by, reading with/to them, setting puzzles, playing board games, cooking together and going on trips. Assist parents to offer their children wise, loving and constructive parenting and to have realistic aspirations.

★ No state funded school to administer its own admissions process, but to admit all pupils from its catchment area, where places exist. End all child selection based on 'faith' or academic ability. Limit parental choice of schooling to local schools i.e. those within a five mile radius of a child's home.

> *'Schools should not be allowed to use academic ability to decide who should be given a place.'*
> (Alliance Party of Northern Ireland Election Manifesto 2005, p.13)

★ All children for whom English is not their first language, to receive extra tuition i.e. after school/Saturdays/school holidays, to enable them to participate fully in the school curriculum as soon as possible.

★ Encourage a germane blend of teaching methods in all schools and reduce computer based learning in favour of creative thinking. Promote the use of Accelerated Learning techniques. Encourage enthusiastic, imaginative and creative teaching in all subjects. Slim down the National Curriculum but maintain it as a framework to ensure that teaching and learning is balanced and consistent in every school, whilst allowing each school to plan and organise teaching and learning in the way that best meets the needs of its pupils.

> *'We will slim down and improve the National Curriculum ... and give teachers the scope once again to be creative and imaginative.'*
> (Conservative Election Manifesto 2005, p.8)

> *'Ensure that creative education is part of the schools curriculum, as well as in all professional, vocational and academic courses.'*
> (Alliance Party of Northern Ireland Election Manifesto 2005, p.24)

★ Guarantee the provision of free, optional, community-based parent/baby 0-2 groups and part-time playgroup places for children aged 2-3 years. Ensure free part-time, school-based nursery places for all children aged 3-4 years and provide statutory part-time pre-school education for all children over four years. All children to commence full-time education in the term after their fifth birthday, attending for half a day for the first half-term.

Abolish school 'breakfast clubs' and end institutional nursery care for children 0-3 years, whilst encouraging informal childcare during the early years through grandparents and childminders.

Review 'Extended Schools' provision with the emphasis being placed on parents and children working together. Existing children's centres to become family centres that provide a range of courses and activities designed to strengthen family relationships and offer parenting support.

> *'The early years of a child's life are critical to their future well-being. But many women who would like to stay at home with their children are forced out into the workplace. Placing their child in a nursery is not their preferred option and denies the fundamental needs of the young child.'*
> (Christian Peoples Alliance Election Manifesto 2005, p.4)

★ Abolish the Early Years Foundation Stage Framework and, instead, encourage natural development and self-discovery through free play. Encourage self-discovery at all ages. Encourage the expansion of toy libraries and reading. All infant classes to be an average of 20 pupils and all junior classes to be an average of 25 pupils. Years 1 and 2 to be foundational years, with teaching focussed on reading, writing and mathematics. All classes in primary/junior schools to have trained non-teaching assistants to work alongside teachers in a supportive role. Encourage the involvement of parents and grandparents in school life. Monitor parental involvement and a child's progress by use of a home/school diary.

> *'Expert opinion confirms what common sense tells us: children well taught and well-cared-for in their early years have a better opportunity to lead successful and rewarding lives ... Liberal Democrats will ... cut infant class sizes ... to an average of 20 and junior class sizes to an average of 25.'*
> (Liberal Democrat Election Manifesto 2005, p.06–07)

★ Limit the exposure of school children to Information and Communication Technology and instead encourage imaginative and creative learning inside and outside the classroom. Assist teachers to encourage children to talk about themselves, to listen to others and to think about the world around them. Give additional funding to small rural primary schools.

MAURICE JONES

'Additional funding for small rural primary schools to enable them to remain viable'
(Sinn Fein Executive Summary 2005, p.4)

★ Bring city academies back into mainstream education and end the development of all-through schools. Integrate grammar schools into the overall school system. Allow grammar schools who do not wish to integrate to become private schools. Private/independent schools to be ineligible for charitable status. Return 'opted out' schools i.e. those with trust status, to local government responsibility. End all business sponsorship of all educational establishments.

★ All state schools to be owned, maintained and repaired by the Unitary District Council.

★ Encourage links between schools, colleges and universities, their local community and the business world. Each school to appoint a teacher with specific responsibility for community liaison. All state schools to run luncheon clubs for local elderly people.

★ Parenting and sex education that promotes sexual abstinence/marriage and a respect for human life to be taught to all children after the age of ten years. 50% of all religious education to be based on the Christian faith. All schools to reflect Christian values i.e. love-the obligation to care for the well-being of others; respect-for all people; patience; justice; commitment; gratefulness; forgiveness; responsibility; joyfulness; humility; honesty and generosity; recognising our own imperfections and not being hypocritical.

School assemblies to be predominantly based on Christian values, with an expectation that all pupils will attend.

'Under the 1944 Education Act, every school may benefit from Christian worship and values. The CPA will ensure every LEA has the resources and expertise to uphold the law in creative and attractive ways that help meet the spiritual needs of children. This will relate to collective worship, Personal, Social, Health and Citizenship Education, relationships and Religious Education.

Schools will be expected to approach the issue of increased under-age pregnancies by promoting the stability offered by marriage and encouraging sexual abstinence. Pupils will be taught the skills and confidence to make right choices, especially when faced by the challenges of alcohol and substance abuse.'
(Christian Peoples Alliance Election Manifesto 2005, p.4)

'The ProLife Alliance is committed to:
Provision of pro-life education which upholds respect for all human life, and affirms the dignity of parents and children.'
(ProLife Alliance Election Manifesto 2005, p.2)

★   Encourage the teaching of a wide variety of sports and creative movement (i.e. various forms of dance) during and after school. Cookery to be taught at all levels of junior/secondary education. Extend the school day by one hour in secondary schools.

Encourage the opening of educational facilities during the evenings and holidays to enable all members of the community to use those facilities.

★   Improve the assessment and clarify the definition of what constitutes a 'special educational need'. Children with special educational needs to be integrated only where appropriate, into mainstream schools with one designated teacher in a small–medium school, but more in larger schools, having responsibility to identify and plan for children with special needs and act as a contact point for parents and other teachers. Increase the number of specialist units attached to mainstream schools and also increase the number of state special schools for children with severe behavioural problems or autistic difficulties, so that appropriate special schooling can be provided as close to their home as possible. Special schools to be linked to research departments in universities and also to act as resource centres to support local schools with their specialist provision. Offer support and guidance to parents of children with special educational needs, as appropriate.

'Children with special educational needs should be schooled in an environment appropriate to their needs - usually in local schools with

appropriate support, or in specialist schools for those who need them. Parents' wishes must be considered when making decisions about type of schooling. A designated teacher in each school will have responsibility to identify and plan for children with special needs, and act as a contact point for parents and other teachers. We will make sure that all teachers and teaching assistants working with children with special educational needs are appropriately trained. Special schools will act as resource centres to support local schools with their specialist provision. In turn special schools will be linked to research departments in universities so that they can benefit directly from, and be involved with, the latest research in special education.'
(Liberal Democrat Election Manifesto 2005, p.06–07)

★ Establish special provision within mainstream schools for 'gifted' children. Remove barriers between academic and vocational training within the secondary school system. Schools to offer all students from the age of 14, in conjunction with local colleges and centres for further education, three paths of learning, either a] study for GCSEs and A-levels, b] combined academic and vocational learning or c] joining a young apprenticeship scheme or learning a trade, a craft or artistic skill.

Review A level and GCSE examinations. Review the benefits of sixth form colleges.

'We will give all students over the age of 14 the opportunity to combine vocational and academic learning …'
(Liberal Democrat Election Manifesto 2005, p.06–07)

'Better training at an earlier age is essential for those less academically-orientated. As a society we must value those with trades such as carpenters, plumbers and electricians.'
(Ulster Democratic Unionist Party Election Manifesto 2005, p.25)

★ End all Standard Assessment Tests. No public exams until Year 10. End 'league tables'.

'Children in England are now the most tested in Europe, yet there is little evidence that … testing and targets has improved standards. Liberal

69

Democrats believe that teachers should be given more time to teach and that testing should have a clear purpose: to improve learning for individual children ... Teachers will regularly assess pupil's performance, using the results to inform teaching and give parents accurate information on their child's progress.'
(Liberal Democrat Election Manifesto 2005, p.06–07)

'we will scrap SATs ...'
(Green Party Election Manifesto 2005, p.16)

★   Comprehensive careers advice and work experience to be given to all older pupils. Those pupils who choose not to pursue further study after leaving school, to receive personalised job-seeking advice in their final term.

★   Head teachers to be enabled to enjoy as much child/staff contact as possible and be the final arbiter with regard to discipline and exclusion. Promote the use of restorative justice by staff in schools dealing with issues such as bullying, truancy, disrespectful behaviour, fighting and petty crime. Encourage parents to respect the authority of teaching staff, particularly with regard to discipline/punishment and also to uphold school policies. Encourage teachers to 'discipline with dignity'.

For pupils who regularly engage in anti-social behaviour or are persistently disruptive, encourage the use of 'positive behaviour plans' and compulsory parenting courses/ legally binding parenting contracts for parents/carers.

Develop Behavioural Exclusion Units to tackle exceptional problems and pupils whose behaviour remains unacceptable. Guarantee support for head teachers who choose to arrange a managed transfer of a pupil to another school or a specialised community initiative that seeks to re-engage children who do not attend or are disruptive in school.

Parents of excluded children to be allowed recourse to an independent appeals panel with the power only to ensure the correct processes were followed, not to overturn the exclusion.

'Children need to learn in a safe and orderly environment, where high standards of behaviour are upheld, where bullying is challenged effectively and where teachers are able to teach without disruption... To deal with

more persistent disruption schools will agree externally monitored 'positive behaviour plans' with parents and pupils.'
(Liberal Democrat Election Manifesto 2005, p.06-07).

★ Ensure anonymity for all teaching staff who are the subject of malicious and unfounded allegations of misconduct, uphold a teacher's legal right to discipline children and reduce the level of paperwork.

'The respect due to teachers will be enhanced by protecting them against malicious allegations of abuse and, most importantly, reducing the massive burden of paperwork.
Children need to be taught how to deal with risks in life. We will encourage learning outside the classroom and provide protection for teachers worried about school trips.'
(Conservative Party Election Manifesto 2005, p.8-9)

★ All children over the age of 16 to undertake a period of community work by participating in local events, clubs and projects during their summer holidays. Discourage companies, particularly those involved in the holiday/leisure industry, from offering discounts/lower prices during the school term. Term-time holidays to be treated as other forms of truancy.

★ Parents who choose to educate their children at home to be regulated via their Unitary District Council and be subject to visits by school inspectors.

★ Expand further education to enable all, at whatever age, to participate in the courses available. Encourage the development of unit-based/modular systems of study. Abolish university tuition and top-up fees and institute maintenance grants for poorer students. End any further expansion of the university sector. Charge the same fees to students from EU countries as are now paid by non-EU students. Review all undergraduate university courses and student grading.

'Liberal Democrats will abolish all tuition fees and make grants available to help poorer students with maintenance costs.'
(Liberal Democrat Election Manifest 2005, p.06-07)

'The UK Independence Party believes that the university sector has already expanded too far. Some courses should be closed releasing funds for those that remain...

Undertake a review of all undergraduate university courses and withdraw funding from those that are of insufficient standard. Fully fund those courses that remain.

Review the standards for grading all courses and ensure that students who do not pass the university's annual examinations are not permitted to continue.

Cancel top-up fees, give maintenance grants as necessary, and scrap the student loan scheme.

Charge the same full fees to students from EU countries as are now paid by non-EU students.'
(UK Independence Party Election Manifesto 2005, p.6)

Increase funding to universities in order to promote research.

'Increase funding for university research projects.'
(Alliance Party of Northern Ireland Election Manifesto 2005, p.14)

★ Ensure that all educational buildings are maintained to a high level.

★ All school inspectors to be employed by the Department of Education. Advisory role of inspectors to be expanded. All schools, colleges, universities and other related educational facilities (including all private educational facilities) to receive random spot checks.

★ Institute one National Examination Board.

★ All schools to have counsellors and school nurses attached. All schools to encourage the wearing of the school uniform until the age of 16 years.

★ Citizenship cards to be issued to those from 5-18 years.

Asylum And Immigration

How we behave towards other people and whether we discriminate for or against them, be they from different ethnic backgrounds, young, old, male or female is largely determined by the attitudes we hold. Attitudes, however, are often best changed not by legislation, but by education and natural interaction at a local level.

The key to good race relations is to help people feel they are part of the local community. The key to community is relationship. The key to relationship is a commitment based on mutual trust, respect and engagement. To enjoy the benefits of community life, all need to contribute to it, be identified with it and have a sense of belonging to it. Minorities become more easily accepted if they are seen as part of the 'whole' For the truth is, when segregation occurs, people become vulnerable to those looking for someone to blame.

There is no doubt that those from different ethnic backgrounds who, in past years have chosen to make the United Kingdom their home, have made a positive contribution in many ways to the life of the nation and therefore xenophobia i.e. a deep dislike of foreigners and racism in all its forms, should be completely repudiated. However, limitless immigration is unsustainable. Every assistance and welcome should be given to genuine asylum seekers/refugees who have experienced or are experiencing physical/emotional abuse or threat because of race, religion, nationality, membership of a particular social/political group and face death or torture. However, leaving country, culture and one's roots can be a traumatic experience. Priority should therefore firstly be given to resolving problems by diplomatic means in those countries where the asylum seekers/refugees originate. Economic migrants are generally hard working and reliable. To describe them, however, as 'cheap labour', or 'fit only to take those jobs the indigenous population will not do' is demeaning, leaves the migrant worker open to abuse and can be used as an excuse for keeping wages low. Also, encouraging those who are highly skilled to leave their country of origin to fill gaps in the UK labour market, only succeeds in weakening that country's efforts to help itself. Emphasis therefore needs to be given to assisting the economic prospects of the countries from which migrant workers originate. There should, in fact, rarely be a need for migrant workers to be employed, as British vacancies should generally be filled by British workers and if this is not the case, the reasons understood and addressed.

* Encourage respect for people in general. Encourage natural diversity whilst promoting integration into society as a whole. Initiate a phased programme of central-government and local-government/public service literature being printed only in the English language. Provide free English language classes for all who are already permanent residents in the United Kingdom and for whom English is not their first language.

* To avoid delay in the processing of applications for asylum, substantially improve the current system. All applicants to be required to have 'just cause' and reasonable identification. Asylum seekers/ refugees to be housed in well resourced reception/support centres whilst their claims are being considered. Those granted temporary asylum to be given British citizenship and residency, with the expectation they will accept assistance to learn the English language, gain a basic knowledge of the country and culture, adhere solely to British democratic values and the law and find employment. Asylum seekers/refugees granted temporary asylum to be able to claim basic State Benefits and be attached to a 'foster family' who are responsible for befriending them and offering practical support. If conditions improve in their country of origin, asylum seekers/refugees to be assisted to return or granted full UK citizenship after five years.

Agree an amnesty for those asylum seekers who have already been resident in the United Kingdom for five years.

'The Christian Peoples Alliance agrees with the late Cardinal Basil Hume when he described protection of those fleeing persecution as a "benchmark of a civilised society". But relatively few refugees seek life and support from prosperous countries. As many people are internally displaced, or live as refugees in neighbouring countries we will ensure help reaches them where they are... Newcomers to Britain will be helped in their understanding and commitment to British democratic values, language and culture.'

(Christian Peoples Alliance Election Manifesto 2005, p.6)

'People fleeing persecution, torture and human rights' violations should always be welcomed by Britain and offered our full protection and asylum. The Green Party is concerned that public debate often confuses the issue of asylum with that of economic migration. Greater public understanding is a key to a sustainable long-term solution.'
(Green Party Election Manifesto 2005, p.30)

'The Christian Peoples Alliance will conduct an overhaul to speed up the process of application and reduce the burden on the appeal system. Justice must work both ways. Unfounded claimants will be returned to the country of their embarkation. There will be no right to automatic settlement and refugees will be helped to return home if conditions in their country improve.'
(Christian Peoples Alliance Election Manifesto 2005, p.6)

'Trevor Phillips, Chair of the Council for Racial Equality, recently said: "multiculturalism is dead ... I believe that once you decide to move to another country, you should embrace the host nation's culture and values".
(Veritas Election Manifesto 2005, The British Way Of Life)

As there will be no right of automatic settlement or right of appeal, asylum seekers/refugees whose claim is refused or who commit a serious offence within five years of obtaining temporary citizenship, will be returned immediately to their country of embarkation/origin.

★   Support the work of the United Nations Refugee Agency in their international action to assist refugees wherever they are and encourage the United Nations to resolve the problems of refugees and asylum seekers within their country of origin. Encourage the establishment of 'safe havens' within countries where conflict exists and guarantee their security with UN peace enforcers.

'... tackling the causes of war and economic injustice - will reduce the need felt by many people to flee long distances as emigrants and refugees. At the same time, we also recognise that immigrants and refugees often make an enormous contribution to the countries and communities they join.'
(Plaid Cymru Election Manifesto 2005, p.16)

'Green policies on issues such as arms sales and unfair trade practices

will reduce the 'push' factors that cause people to leave their country of origin.'
(Green Party Election Manifesto 2005, p.30)

★   Enforce the strict screening of potential criminal suspects entering and leaving Britain.

Robustly combat people trafficking and the abuse of women and children by prosecuting those involved in the 'sex industry'.

'Reinstate embarkation controls to check those entering and leaving Britain. It is essential to keep proper records of those crossing our borders.'
(UK Independence Party Election Manifesto 2005, p.7)

'What will we do?
Allow judges to jail people-smugglers for life and seize their assets'
(Veritas Election Manifesto 2005, Asylum)

'We will combat the criminal trafficking and sexual abuse of women and children by coming down hard on those controlling so-called 'sex industries.'
(Christian Peoples Alliance Election Manifesto 2005, p.6)

★   Manage economic migration by a) migrants having a specific job to come to, b) an agreed date of departure.

Economic migrants to have access during their stay to basic healthcare i.e. a GP/Accident and Emergency, but no entitlement to benefits.

Economic migrants who enter the country illegally, or without reasonable documentation, or who commit an offence, to be immediately deported to their country of origin/embarkation. Increase the penalties for those employers who knowingly employ illegal economic migrants. Economic migrants from EU and non-EU countries to be treated equally and, those who have been working in the UK for less than three years to be asked to leave the country within six months with assistance offered to help them relocate.

★   Ensure a stricter control of residence rights granted because of family connections.

★ Balance national security with the protection of individual civil liberties.

Housing

The Government has a responsibility to ensure those who are without a home receive appropriate assistance by providing not only temporary accommodation for those who choose to live on the fringes of society, but also long-term housing that meets the needs of every level of society.

In recent years, owner-occupied houses and flats have come to be viewed as 'assets' rather than homes, a way of making money rather than providing a place to live. That perception needs to change and stability restored to the housing market.

A home is one of the basic necessities of life, enabling people to live independently and allowing them the opportunity to create their own personal environment. The housing stock therefore needs to be as varied as possible, but with the emphasis being on obtaining rather than owning a home.

As new houses use up valuable land and other natural resources, environmental concerns need to be given a high priority. Thus the emphasis should be on the renovation of older properties and buildings, with all new housing, planner - rather than developer -led. Where new house building is allowed, low cost social (council) housing should have priority, with housing developments concentrated in urban locations and on 'brownfield' sites with no new building for whatever reason on designated Green Belt land. Bad design is wasteful, boring and often impracticable. Therefore all new buildings, whether commercial or domestic, should be designed to be practical in terms of use and also visually stimulating.

★ Ensure a greater investment in social (council) housing/flat building (with no right to buy) through Unitary District Councils. Council rents to meet the cost of management and maintenance and also to pay for the original cost of the property over its lifetime. Homeowners who are in danger of being repossessed to be given the option of selling their property at auction value to the Unitary

District Council and remain on a rented basis with the choice of buying the property back if their circumstances improve. Enable Unitary District Councils to purchase private-builders' unsold homes. Return all Housing Association properties to local government control whilst ensuring tenants have a greater role in decision-making about their homes and neighbourhood. Encourage shared ownership and leasehold arrangements for key workers and first time buyers, particularly in rural areas and the provision of rented 'starter homes'.

★ Enforce the protection of all Green Belt land from building and establish more Green Belts. All Unitary District Councils to initiate within their area an audit and, if necessary, the compulsory purchase at auction value of all long-term unoccupied properties, with a view to adding to the housing stock and the conversion of old redundant buildings for residential or mixed use. Also, to identify unused development areas i.e. all brownfield sites and redundant Ministry of Defence/NHS land with approaches made to landowners, whether public or private, to deliver new build. Permission already granted for building on all green field sites and flood plains to be withdrawn with provision being made for financial compensation where building work has already begun. Planning permission to be given only on the basis that the development will primarily consist of social, affordable housing and, in villages, only on infill sites within the village envelope, with applicants demonstrating a genuine local connection.

> 'The CPA will take a radical and innovative approach to the national shortage of housing. Unused development areas will be identified and land owners, whether public or private, approached to deliver significant new build. We shall also promote shared-equity schemes and leasehold arrangements where key workers can buy homes but not land on which they are built, so making property more affordable. Empty homes will be brought back into use and buildings converted to residential or mixed use … Developers must … not equate affordable housing with just semi-detached or detached solutions.'
>
> (Christian Peoples Alliance Election Manifesto 2005, p.8)

'We will promote development on brownfield sites and establish more Green Belts with tighter development rules.'
(Conservative Party Election Manifesto 2005, p.22-23)

★ Ensure that private rented sector tenants are adequately protected within the law.

'The SSP stands for: The transformation of our housing schemes, using environmental artists, landscape gardeners and others with relevant skills to help turn our housing schemes into pleasant places to live. Proper tenant representation for private rented sector tenants.'
(Scottish Socialist Party Election Manifesto 2005, p.41)

★ Restrict new house building in the Southeast of England, whilst seeking to promote house building in other parts of the country, particularly in the North and the Southwest. Reassess the four successful bids for 'eco-towns' with a view to limiting their size or abandoning them altogether.

★ Encourage flexibility and variety in mortgage provision and the use of Home Income Plans for the elderly. Second homes which are unoccupied for 75% of the year to be sold. Houses that are purchased on a buy-to-let basis to be registered with the Unitary District Council with owners ensuring a 90% yearly occupancy. Encourage mutual respect between gypsy/traveller families and landowners. Provide adequate long-term rented local authority sites with hard-standing pitches and toilet facilities for gypsy/traveller families. Encourage gypsies/travellers to build community links and meaningfully contribute to the wider society. Evict gypsy/traveller families or anyone who illegally occupies private or council owned land or breaches planning laws, without the right to appeal.

'We will... give new powers to help local councils to deal with those incidents, such as illegal traveller encampments, which breach planning laws.'
(Conservative Party Election Manifesto 2005, p.22)

'What will we do? evict travellers promptly if they occupy sites illegally,

require travellers to be subject to our criminal and planning laws like everyone else, make it a criminal offence for travellers to occupy land without permission - thus ensuring that they can be removed immediately from land they've occupied without permission - and charged with a criminal offence, reinstate the duty on local authorities to build enough sites for travellers - always providing that travellers are charged an economic rent for using them.'
(Veritas Election Manifesto 2005, Travellers)

★ Develop a multi-agency approach to tackle homelessness. Provide adequate hostel/night shelter accommodation for those who are homeless and choose to live on the streets and assist those who wish, to return to mainstream living. Encourage the development of YMCA hostels and housing for young people.

'Development of a statutory multi-agency approach to tackle … homelessness. This should have preventative, innovative and flexible approaches.'
(Sinn Fein Executive Summary 2005, p.6)

★ Ensure that those who are elderly are assisted to improve their homes with the installation of suitable aids, insulation and heating and alarm systems. Encourage the development of local authority 'care and repair' schemes. All new housing to be designed with life-long needs in mind and a considered percentage to be made fully accessible for wheelchair users.

'Winter mortality rates amongst the elderly are unacceptable and avoidable. The DUP Warm Homes Scheme has brought new heating systems to thousands of homes and insulation measures to many thousands more.'
(Ulster Democratic Unionist Party Election Manifesto 2005, p.27)

'All new public housing to be designed to meet life-long needs.'
(Sinn Fein Executive Summary 2005, p.7)

★ Require developers to prove that any housing/commercial development will benefit the local community and environment and that sufficient consideration has been given to the provision of the necessary infrastructure, particularly public transport. Substantially limit the number of 'out of town' shopping developments.

'The SSP stands for: No more planning permission for out-of-town shops which encourage car use.'
(Scottish Socialist Party Election Manifesto 2005, p.20)

'Planning policies to encourage public transport access for shopping centres, leisure facilities, and housing developments. When public services such as post offices and courts are closed, as well as causing inconvenience, that also has the effect of generating increased traffic.'
(Plaid Cymru Election Manifesto 2005, p.12)

'Ensure necessary infrastructure is put in place before new major housing developments commence. For example, sufficient consideration must be given to potential new residents' access to public transport.'
(Alliance Party of Northern Ireland Election Manifesto 2005, p.17)

★ Encourage the construction of buildings using renewable building materials such as wood. Review the benefits of Home Information Packs. Encourage neighbours to work together to improve their neighbourhood.Encourage creative ways to revitalise empty shops. Encourage community ownership of facilities.

Transport

The Government has a responsibility to develop a consistent national transport strategy and the long-term planning of the nation's infrastructure.

The future of transport in the United Kingdom lies in achieving a balance between environmentally friendly private motoring, public transport that is reliable, convenient, integrated and cheaper than other forms of transport and the efficient non-polluting movement of freight. Also, to generally reduce the need to travel, whilst promoting cycling and walking, thereby giving cognisance to the overall health of the nation. At present, commercial aircraft are not only noisy, but highly pollutant and the infra-structure required for inland airports wasteful in terms of land use. Until such times as aircraft manufacturers are able to produce pollutant free, silent aircraft, growth in air travel should be substantially reduced.

'Our transport systems have been built to solve the wrong problem. Successive governments have tried to deal with the increasing demand for mobility by spending billions of pounds on transport plans that give us more of the same - more roads, wider motorways, more runways. Real progress on transport requires us to tackle the root causes of demand for mobility.

The Green approach is to review how we plan and structure our towns and cities, and to give priority to more sustainable modes of transport. This approach favours the public over the private, and ranks modes of transport in the following hierarchy: walking; cycling; trains; rail freight; trams and buses; road freight; private car… The aim is to encourage a wide-scale shift from car, lorry and air use to other, more sustainable, modes of transport.' (Green Party Election Manifesto 2005, p.17)

★ Rail network to be part owned by the Government and part owned by employee shareholders. Substantially increase public investment in the rail system throughout the UK, particularly in the provision of more seats, opening new lines and reopening lines closed by Dr Beeching. Also, to replace older parts of the network including track and bridges, improve day to day maintenance and ensure the costs of operating and running the network safely are fully met. Establish a national high-speed electrified inter-city rail network.

Upgrade all stations and ensure that the London Crossrail and Thameslink projects are completed as soon as possible. Expand the rail freight network and safeguard the land adjacent to railways in order to develop freight interchange/distribution centres.

'…we will encourage the development of freight interchanges to facilitate growth in rail freight…'
(Liberal Democrat Election Manifesto 2005, p.16-17)

'The SSP stands for: A vast expansion of rail, involving the reopening of old railway lines and stations closed down in the days before the threat of road congestion and carbon emissions were fully understood.

Faster, cheaper and more frequent ferry and rail services to shift passenger traffic from air to rail and sea to help curb pollution.'
(Scottish Socialist Party Election Manifesto 2005, p.26-27)

'Plaid Cymru … wants to see: 'Privatisation of the railways reversed …''
(Plaid Cymru Election Manifesto 2005, p.12)

'Secure and expand the railway system in Northern Ireland.'
(Alliance Party of Northern Ireland Election Manifesto 2005, p.19)

'The Green Party believes that the fragmentation of the rail and tube systems and the introduction of artificial competition has been a strategic failure and we do not believe the Government's plans for restructuring the railways will solve the problems. We will not renew the private-sector train operating companies' contracts when they are due for franchise renewal. Instead, we will return the railways and tube system, including both track and operations, to public ownership. In transport planning the Green Party will:
Give higher priority to railways and introduce new lines
Expand the rail freight network
Open additional stations on existing routes
Safeguard land adjacent to railways for use in freight distribution projects'
(Green Party Election Manifesto 2005, p.18)

Invest in light rail/tram systems within cities. Develop monorail cross-country links.

London Underground to be publicly owned. Initiate go anywhere tickets for use on buses, rail and coaches and generally integrate all transport ticketing systems. Substantially lower the price of rail tickets.

★ Encourage the pedestrianisation of large towns and cities and the use of bicycles and electric bikes via an expansion of safe, well-maintained and well-lit cycle tracks. Pursue research into making cyclists less vulnerable when on public roads, particularly from HGVs.

'The SSP stands for: An extensive network of safe, well-maintained and well-lit cycle tracks.'
(Scottish Socialist Party Election Manifesto 2005, p.26)

'More attention to the needs of cyclists and pedestrians, such as cycle tracks and safe routes to school.'
(Plaid Cymru Election Manifesto 2005, p.12)

★   Promote research into hydrogen fuel cell/electric powered cars and buses.

'Investment in and research into the use of less-polluting fuels,'
(Plaid Cymru Election Manifesto 2005, p.12)

★   All new vehicles to be fitted with a 'tracker' homing device. Institute a no drink/drug driving policy.

To discourage short journeys by car, replace the current Road Tax system by placing Road Tax onto the price of petrol. Increase the penalties for driving without a current MOT or valid insurance. Substantially raise the purchase tax on fuel-inefficient cars and those with high pollutant emissions. Expand low cost park-and-ride schemes.

'The SSP stands for:
Expansion of low cost park-and-ride schemes.'
(Scottish Socialist Party Election Manifesto 2005, p.26)

'Work to reduce numbers of small journeys by car through better planning and schemes to end the 'school run.'
(Green Party Election Manifesto 2005, p.17-18)

★   Encourage the development of a frequent, low cost, long-distance, integrated national coach network. Increase the level of midi/mini bus services and country cars in rural areas with interconnected routes and timetables. Develop Post Bus services. Generally improve and expand bus services in urban/city areas through more dedicated bus lanes, cross-city bus routes and integrated timetables and encourage businesses to promote car sharing and assist their employees to embrace environmentally friendly commuting.

* Encourage people to work from home using computer based technology.

> *'Greater investment in bus services in rural areas.'*
> (Plaid Cymru Election Manifesto 2005, p.12)

> *'The Green Party will act to reduce our dependency on the motor car by planning to reduce demand and by provision of a viable alternative in the form of high quality, safe and reliable public transport systems.*
>
> *Intelligent planning can also promote better use of existing roads through bus lanes, car sharing schemes and commuter plans. The Green Party will:*
> *Assist businesses with greener commuting arrangements for staff.'*
> (Green Party Election Manifesto 2005, p.17-18)

> *'Improve public transport, through the increase in park and ride schemes, more dedicated bus lanes, cross-city bus routes, better integrated timetables, and more efficient fare collection systems.'*
> (Alliance Party of Northern Ireland Election Manifesto 2005, p.19)

* All major road building projects to be reappraised. Road freight to use specifically designated roads. Upper limit of 50 mph on all rural single carriageway roads.

> *'We will not proceed with major new road-building schemes unless the benefits are clear, including environmental and safety factors and a full assessment of alternative public transport schemes.'*
> (Liberal Democrat Election Manifesto 2005, p.16-17)

Improve the co-ordination of road works and ensure repairs and maintenance are completed quickly and with minimum inconvenience to road users. Ensure utility and communication companies who dig up the roads, repair them to a satisfactory level.

> *'Improve the co-ordination of road works, and boost the repair and maintenance of roads. ... We must not neglect our roads but ensure they*

are maintained to a high standard. Utilities and communication companies who dig up our roads must repair them to a satisfactory level.'
(Alliance Party of Northern Ireland Election Manifesto 2005, p.19)

★   Minimum age for driving a moped 17 years. Minimum age for holding a provisional driving license 19 years. Newly qualified drivers to have a two year probationary period and be limited to driving low cc cars after which, following satisfactory completion, a full license to be granted. Three yearly driving tests for those over 70 years. Twenty year 'refresher' driving tests for all other drivers. Free nationwide travel on public transport for those over 65 years.

'It was the DUP who were responsible for the introduction of free travel on public transport for the over 65s. We recognised older people are less likely to have their own car and rely more heavily on public transport for necessities such as shopping and medical appointments, and to provide a lifeline to the outside world.'
(Ulster Democratic Unionist Party Election Manifesto 2005, p.26)

★   Close Stansted Airport and use the land for light industry/housing. Review the expansion of all other airports. Plans for a third runway at Heathrow to be cancelled. A new international airport to be built off the coast of East Anglia or in the Thames Gateway. Substantially increase the air passenger duty on all domestic/European short-haul flights.
    Ban night flying to all inland airports and all aircraft to be stacked off-shore.

'Air transport is a major, and growing, source of greenhouse gas emissions … We will work to shift shorter air journeys to the railways…, resist further expansion of UK airports and ban night flying.'
(Green Party Election Manifesto 2005, p.18)

★   Seek to reduce harmful emissions from shipping and expand regional ports to shorten the distance containers need to travel overland.

Justice

For any society not to decline into anarchy, the judicial system must be seen to be 'just' and those paid to enforce the law to be, as far as is possible, above reproach.

Imprisoning people is expensive and prisons often act as 'universities of crime'. Although prisons will always be necessary for those who have committed serious crimes, the focus needs to be on developing alternatives to institutional imprisonment particularly for children and young people.

It is right that those in prison should loose their liberty, but retain their dignity. Those imprisoned, therefore, should be humanely treated, allowed basic necessities and human rights, be provided with useful employment and education and detained as near to their homes as possible. There should be no early release however for 'good behaviour', the expectation being that prisoners while serving their sentence naturally behave well. Assistance should be given to enable offenders to practically recompense society for their crimes, with the emphasis being not only on punishment but also rehabilitation thereby reducing the unacceptably high rates of re-offending.

Restorative justice, which gives victims of crime who want it the chance to tell offenders the real impact of their offending and offenders the chance to apologise and turn their lives around, should be promoted not only in the criminal justice setting and prisons, but also by those dealing with conflict in the community. The essence, then, of crime reduction is not simply locking people up, but encouraging a high regard and respect for people at all levels of society, with the police not being anonymous agents of law enforcement, but intrinsic members of their local community, working to build relationships and promote crime prevention. It may or may not be that society is becoming more violent, but the priority should always be on understanding the reasons behind the violence and dealing with them, rather than using ever more draconian and expensive measures to stop any violence that occurs.

Crime and anti-social behaviour usually have their roots in a) family breakdown, b) unemployment or c) a victim culture, where offenders blame society for their circumstances, do not believe they can change their behaviour and are generally unwilling to take responsibility for their actions. Offending by young people is often seen as a means of raising your 'street cred', enjoying the companionship and comradeship that 'gang culture' offers or earning a living. As enforcement alone will not stop youth crime, emphasis needs to be given to developing in children and young people, attitudes of self-respect and respect for other people, which stem from high self-esteem, self-worth, skills that will benefit themselves and society and a removing of a sense of exclusion.

Effective crime prevention on the streets, then, begins not in the school, or in the youth club or in the police station, but in the home. Children are not born criminals. Children behave badly because of negative influences in their early life. Violence in the home, physical or mental, often leads to violence on the streets. Melanie Phillips comments,

> 'The biggest reason for the rise in crime is the relentless growth of a lethal sub-culture of fatherless children and disorderly homes. While many lone parents do a good job of bringing up their children, the fact remains that most delinquents have fractured family lives.
>
> There are whole communities where committed fathers are unknown. As a result, the process of socialising children has broken down, leading to youngsters from emotionally chaotic backgrounds violently acting out their disturbance in school before being sucked into crime.
>
> The truth is that the family is the crucible of social order. Break the family, and you break social order. How can children respect their parents when at the deepest level they believe that their parents have abandoned them? Such abandonment makes children feel they are worthless. If they don't even respect themselves, how can they be expected to respect authority?'

Although most single parents work hard to love, care for and support their children, separation and divorce is painful for adults and without proper management can be emotionally destructive for children. If mediation cannot bring about some resolution to the difficulties a couple may be facing and their relationship is dissolved, it is crucial that they understand parenthood is not dissoluble and that children need, and usually want, both their mother and their father to be actively involved in their lives, as long as each parent is a positive influence and there are no concerns about child abuse or violence.

Thus, rather than one parent having overall custody of a child/children, emphasis needs to be given towards the encouragement of shared parenting – not equal time necessarily, although that may be an option that can work for some children – but parenting arrangements that allow both parents an opportunity to be actively involved in their children's daily routines as far as is possible. That allows children to have the meaningful involvement of both parents on a continuous basis.

One of the great strengths of British policing has been the willingness of officers to remain unarmed except in specific circumstances and to carry out their duties with the minimum use of force. These principles need to be actively pursued in general policing so as to discourage responding to aggression with aggression. In order to be fully effective in crime investigation/resolution, on a local and national level, police forces need to work collaboratively across county boundaries whenever necessary and be comprehensively resourced.

Crime is not solely the problem of the government or the police. We all have a responsibility to limit its influence.

Free Speech is the hallmark of a democratic society and a safeguard against dictatorship. We should all have the right to say what we believe. But equally, we all have a responsibility to think before we say it. Any individual or group that responds with violence or intimidation when criticised demonstrates they have something to hide.

'… the largest impact on crime will come from … job opportunities, reforming education, restoring local democracy, and reinforcing family values. With a greater sense of purpose and belonging, the crime problem will become easier to manage, even drug-related crime and the anti-social behaviour associated with binge-drinking.'
(UK Independence Party Election Manifesto 2005, p.7)

'We will support the social institutions - families, schools, voluntary bodies and youth clubs - that can prevent crime and drug dependency before it starts.'
(Conservative Party Election Manifesto 2005, p.16)

★ Ensure the development of community based crime prevention and reduction measures. Improve the design of cities and towns to provide safer streets and public places and ensure universal access to high quality youth facilities and the prompt repair of damage done to public amenities and spaces.

★ Repeal the legislation relating to the introduction of ID cards for UK citizens.

> 'The Green Party will develop and invest in a range of crime reduction and prevention measures that focus on tackling local sources of potential crime and improving the safety of our communities. These measures will address the social and environmental causes of crime and will include:
> Improving the design of our cities to provide safer streets and public spaces
> Ensuring universal access to high quality youth facilities
> Repairing damage done to public amenities and spaces promptly
> Opposing national ID cards, which will not reduce or prevent crime'
> (Green Party Election Manifesto 2005, p.24)

> 'What will we do?
>
> … refuse to introduce Identity Cards, which won't reduce crime, fraud, terrorism or illegal immigration, but will cost a fortune and give the state too many powers.'
> (Veritas Election Manifesto 2005, Civil Liberties)

★ Encourage the growth of Neighbourhood Watch Schemes and Neighbourhood Action Groups, which consist of people who live and work in a neighbourhood and those who provide a service to the local community, meeting on a regular basis, to agree community priorities and realistic/achievable courses of action.

Enhance neighbourhood policing by increasing the number and visibility of uniformed police officers/foot and pedal cycle patrols and special constables in neighbourhood teams. Reopen local police stations. Encourage police officers to build community links i.e. by regularly visiting schools, daycentres and to be actively involved in community youth schemes.

Promote the use of restorative justice in conflict situations in the local community.

'Restitution for the victim and the community and rehabilitation of the offender are key ingredients of the Green approach to justice.
Link crime reduction to strong local communities
Support and increase community policing
Introduce restorative justice'
(Green Party Election Manifesto 2005, p.24)

★ Improve the training and selection of police. Minimum age of entry 22 years.

★ Support the presumption of innocence for homeowners defending their homes from intruders and those who make a citizen's arrest or act in good faith to prevent a crime.

'Support the presumption of innocence for homeowners defending their homes from intruders.'
(UK Independence Party Election Manifesto 2005, p. 7)

★ Relieve police of all unnecessary paperwork/targets.

'Cut the bureaucracy that keeps police officers desk bound 50% of the time.'
(Plaid Cymru Election Manifesto 2005, p.14)

'We need to relieve our forces from too much central direction, including performance targets, the mass of paperwork and politically-correct rules that ignore the realities of the job.'
(UK Independence Party Election Manifesto 2005, p.7)

★ Maintain an independent police complaints authority.

'The SSP stands for: An independent police complaints authority.'
(Scottish Socialist Party Election Manifesto 2005, p.47)

★ Develop a co-ordinated, national, multi-agency approach towards investigating internationally organised crime e.g. large scale drug importation, kidnap and fraud, through well resourced intelligence, analysis and enforcement. Ensure police forces have adequate resources to effectively undermine the activities of local criminal gangs and establish, nationwide, Violence Reduction Units based on the project currently run by Strathclyde Police that seeks to engage with gang members and, if they change their ways, to offer them an alternative to police action. Fully enforce the law relating to joint enterprise, where anyone caught up in a serious incident could face the same jail sentence as the perpetrator.

★ Increase the sentencing power of magistrates and reopen local magistrate courts.

Broaden the selection of magistrates and encourage consistency in sentencing for all offences, but ensure that crimes against people are treated with more severity than crimes against property and profit. Maintain the discretion of a judge to allow the presence of the media in court. Improve access to Legal Aid whilst closely monitoring its effectiveness. Develop and encourage the use of the small claims court. Uphold the right to trial by jury.

Encourage flexible 'life' sentences for murder with intent, ranging from a minimum of 30 years, to a maximum of 80 years without remission. All other prisoners to serve the full sentence handed down by the court. Seek to recover assets gained by illegal means, from convicted criminals, and use them to fund community projects.

'We will introduce honesty in sentencing so that criminals serve the full sentence handed down by the court.'
(Conservative Party Election Manifesto 2005, p.16)

All prisoners to be assessed with regard to their long-term needs. Provide full-time education, training and employment for all prisoners and institute minimum national standards of care in all prisons. Promote the use of restorative justice within prisons with regard to helping victims, resolving inmates' complaints, restoring calm in volatile situations and tackling repeat offenders' deep-rooted problems. Ensure comprehensive prisoner-release programmes and the close monitoring of any offender returning to the community by expanding and developing the role of the Probation Service.

'With four out of five prisoners functionally illiterate, and over half of prisoners re-offending, it's time to make prison work. Prisoners will be subject to a tough working day, with increased resources for education and training a top priority so that they learn the skills to acquire a legitimate job.'
(Liberal Democrat Election Manifesto 2005, p.08–09)

'Half of offenders go on to recommit crime. We propose radical solutions within the Prison Service by tackling repeat offenders' deep rooted problems, such as by the introduction of restorative justice programmes... Backing will be given to prisoner-release and family support networks.'
(Christian Peoples Alliance Election Manifesto 2005, p.8)

'Use restorative justice and community sentencing, where appropriate, so that the criminal contributes back to society.'
(Plaid Cymru Election Manifesto 2005, p.14)

★   All prisons to be built, managed and fully funded by the state.

'The SSP stands for: Opposition to privatisation and PFI in the prison service and for private jails to be brought back into public ownership.'
(Scottish Socialist Party Election Manifesto 2005, p.48)

Reduce the overall prison building programme. Any new building to focus on smaller, local prisons.

★   Expand the use of non-custodial sentences, particularly for those under 18 years who commit non-violent crimes, by providing comprehensive rehabilitation facilities within the community. Develop meaningful, demanding, community service for persistent young offenders. Encourage the development of family courts and increase parental responsibility for non-violent young offenders. Encourage the development of a) activities for young people during the school holidays, b) mentoring schemes for young people excluded from school and who offend, c) obligatory parenting courses for parents of children with criminal convictions and d) befriending networks.

'Liberal Democrats will make more non-violent criminals - such as fine

defaulters, shoplifters and petty vandals - do tough community work as an alternative to jail. Experience shows that this reduces re-offending, gives them skills for legitimate work, and means that they pay back the community.'
(Liberal Democrat Election Manifesto 2005, p.08-09)

★   Promote the long-term support of all victims of crime, witnesses and families of offenders and those who suffer sexual violence/domestic abuse particularly children and women. Support both statutory and community projects that help victims build a shared sense of healing and recovery. Substantially invest in a national infrastructure of refuges and organisations to support women and men suffering from abuse and/or violence and adopt a zero tolerance response towards those who commit such offences.

'The SSP stands for: Full funding to services which support women - and men - who have suffered violence, abuse, rape and child sexual abuse. More women's refuges and safe housing.'
(Scottish Socialist Party Election Manifesto 2005, p.33)

'Provide greater support for victims and witnesses to help people feel safer in their communities.'
(Plaid Cymru Election Manifesto 2005, p.13)

'Mainstream funding for frontline and community services which support women and children affected by violence.'
(Sinn Fein Executive Summary 2005, p.5)

'Support both statutory and community projects that help victims build a shared sense of healing and recovery. Ensure that adequate funding is put in place for victims' organisations.'
(Alliance Party of Northern Ireland Election Manifesto 2005, p.10)

★   Provide readily available pre and post-marriage guidance. Encourage the development of Family Centres which offer free mediation between parents, support services to prevent relationship breakdown and a neutral venue in which divorced parents can see their children. Neutral conciliation and mediation to be mandatory for married couples with children who divorce or cohabiting couples with children who separate.

Uncontested divorces to be allowed after two years separation. Divorces to be considered on a 'joint fault' basis. Three years separation to be required where only one partner wants the divorce. Ensure that all decisions taken which affect children's lives are always taken in the best interests of the child. Ensure a significant national level of provision for children in and leaving care.

'Ensure all decisions taken which affect children's lives are taken in the best interests of the child.'
(Sinn Fein Executive Summary 2005, p.5)

★ Ensure a co-ordinated government response to terrorism in all its forms by providing adequate funding for the intelligence services, training for the emergency services, controlled immigration and rigorous arrangements for the extradition and deportation of terrorist subjects.

'A Conservative Government will place the highest possible priority on combating the threat from terrorism. This requires a co-ordinated response right across government, including funding for the intelligence services, training for the emergency services ... controlled immigration and rigorous arrangements for the extradition and deportation of terrorist suspects.'
(Conservative Party Election Manifesto 2005, p.16)

'Terrorism is not the way, terrorism is not the way. It doesn't beget peace. We can't deliver peace by terrorism, never can we deliver peace by killing people. Throughout history, those people who have changed the world have done so without violence; they have won people to their cause through peaceful protest. Nelson Mandela, Martin Luther King, Mahatma Gandhi: their discipline, their self-sacrifice, their conviction made people turn towards them, to follow them. What inspiration can senseless slaughter provide? Death and destruction of young people in their prime as well as the old and helpless can never be the foundations for building society.'
(Marie Fatayi-Williams whose son Anthony was killed in the London bombings on 7th July 2005).

★ Oppose hatred, physical violence or verbal abuse against anyone but promote the right to peaceful public protest and free speech including the right to publicly question the activities of faith groups. Uphold the right of all political/social groups to, within the law, voice their opinions and faith groups to express their faith-based views.

Freedom of speech and thought and freedom of conscience and belief are an absolute right. We should therefore always ensure we do not destroy what we are trying to protect, i.e. our liberty in these areas, by restrictive legislation.

'What will we do?
Stand for and defend freedom of speech and thought, freedom of conscience and belief.'
(Veritas Election Manifesto 2005, Civil Liberties)

Energy

The Government has a responsibility to guarantee the security and sustainability of Britain's energy supplies by combining a mix of energy sources thereby ensuring that the nation's energy needs are fully met in an environmentally friendly way and at a price that reduces energy demand.

There is no doubt that the world's resources of oil and gas are steadily declining and the importation of energy may not, in the long-term, be secure. If future generations are to avoid energy impoverishment, the aim should be to expand research into all viable methods of energy production so as to make the nation as energy self-sufficient as possible and also to discourage wasteful consumption. The decommissioning of nuclear power stations is likely to be a costly burden for years to come. Atomic energy should not therefore be pursued until such times as its overall costs can be substantially reduced.

★ Ensure all new houses meet strict energy-efficiency targets. Promote a national insulation program for all existing buildings.

MAURICE JONES

> *'We… recognise that energy efficiency must play an increasingly important role in our energy policy.'*
> (Conservative Party Election Manifesto 2005, p.23)

Extend minimum guarantee periods to encourage the repair of goods rather than their replacement.

★   Accelerate research and development into 'clean coal' technology i.e. carbon capture and storage technology (CCS) with all existing coal-fired power stations being fitted with CCS as soon as possible. End opencast mining on all green field sites and review opencast mining on brownfield sites, but explore the reopening of British deep mines, with a view to increasing coal-fired generation.

★   Maintain the development of offshore wind farms/wave /tidal-stream power, particularly with a view to exporting the technology. End the building of onshore wind farms. Accelerate research and development into all forms of renewable energy sources, e.g. solar thermal power that uses parabolic mirrors to reflect the sun's rays to generate heat and electricity, whilst being sensitive and selective about where renewable energy development is sited.

> *'A Conservative Government will guarantee the security and sustainability of Britain's energy supplies. We will do this by supporting the development of a broad range of renewable energy sources.'*
> (Conservative Election Manifesto 2005, p.23)

> *'Renewable energy sources – including energy from the sun, tides, wind, water, and energy crops – are far more benign for the environment and world peace, and cannot run out.'*
> (Plaid Cymru Election Manifesto 2005, p.17)

Encourage the development of 'micro-generation', particularly through solar PV (photovoltaic) technology and personal wind turbines, and enable consumers to feed excess power from 'micro-generation' back into an upgraded/expanded National Grid network.

Encourage research into nuclear power generation whilst decommissioning all current nuclear power stations as they come to the end of their life. End all plans for new nuclear power stations.

> 'We do not accept the argument that only through the expansion of nuclear power can we hope to solve the energy and climate change problem. The hidden costs of nuclear power ... are huge.
>
> We will decommission all nuclear power stations as they come to the end of their life.' (Green Party Election Manifesto 2005, p.10)

Substantially increase gas storage and ensure gas-fired power stations are as 'carbon clean' as possible.

* Encourage consumers to conserve gas and electricity by operating a pay structure that has an initial flat rate, after which, the more you use the more you pay. Tax high energy household items, where there is a low energy alternative.

All homes to be fitted with a 'smart meter' to provide customers with relevant and actionable information regarding their gas and electricity usage, with the cost of installation being shared equally between the government and the customer.

> 'As part of the plans to reduce emissions we will implement strategies to reduce domestic and business energy usage. These strategies will focus on reducing energy demand as well as increasing overall efficiency.'
> (Green Party Election Manifesto 2005, p.10)

* Re-establish a controlling interest by government in the electricity generation and supply industry by purchasing 51% of the shares. All new high voltage cables to be placed underground.

Broadcasting, Films And The Media

Any organisation or individual that has the opportunity by word, print or picture to influence other individuals, must always ensure that their information is correct and is presented clearly and without bias, despite the personal opinions held by the journalist/editor. To report what is factual, rather than what is sensational. Also, that the organisation or individual recognise their responsibility to maintain high standards of decency and seek to achieve a balance between the individual's right to privacy and the public's 'right to know'.

What people watch, listen to or read affects their attitudes, values and behaviour, particularly in their formative years. Those who prepare and deliver television programmes/films/literature therefore have a responsibility to consider the general welfare of the age group they are seeking to communicate with and the overall community. The emphasis then should be on quality rather than quantity of output, so that the 'best' is not sacrificed on the altar of the 'more'. Consideration therefore needs to be given to reducing overall broadcasting output to avoid the making of programmes that simply fill up the schedule.

To ensure impartial reporting all media outlets should be free from political interference and manipulation.

Carved in marble in the entrance hall of BBC Broadcasting House at Portland Place in London is a Latin inscription inspired by verses in 2 Corinthians 15 and Philippians 4 which should serve to underpin the output of all public service broadcasting:

'To Almighty God, This Temple of the Arts and Muses is dedicated to Almighty God by the first Governors of Broadcasting in the year 1931, Sir John Reith being Director-General. It is their prayer that good seed sown may bring forth a good harvest, that all things hostile to peace or purity may be banished from this house, and that the people, inclining their ear to whatsoever things are beautiful and honest and of good report, may tread the path of wisdom and uprightness'.

★ To ensure the long-term editorial independence of the BBC, maintain the traditional system of multi-year funding agreements with the licence fee money being used solely for projects connected with the BBC's public purposes.

Licence fee to be set by an Independent Licence Review Body. Encourage the BBC:

a) To inform, educate and entertain
b) To serve everyone and enrich people's lives
c) To be the most creative, trusted organisation in the world

d) To manage its services adequately to ensure value for money to the licence fee payer
e) Ensure all staff uphold standards of common decency when broadcasting
f) Ensure that programming is of the highest quality and original.

★ Appoint an independent, external regulator appointed by Parliament, to monitor all public service broadcasting.

> *'The BBC has, over the last eighty years, made a major contribution to Britain's democracy, culture and standing in the world. The Liberal Democrats will make sure it remains the world's leading public service broadcaster - strong, independent, and securely funded. But the regulation of the BBC has been insufficiently independent of its own management, and of the Government … Liberal Democrats will … introduce a new, independent external regulator appointed by Parliament, to make sure that all public service broadcasters live up to their obligations to the public.'*
> (Liberal Democrat Election Manifesto 2005, p.18-19)

★ Encourage all commercial networks to deliver programmes of high quality. Free TV licences for those aged 65 and above.

> *'The DUP has campaigned for free television licences for older people. We recognise that the elderly rely heavily on TV for services and information. We therefore believe that free TV licences should be provided to all older people aged 65 and above.'*
> (Ulster Democratic Unionist Party Election Manifesto 2005, p.27)

★ All major sporting events i.e. Wimbledon, FA Cup final, the Derby/Grand National etc. and competitions that involve national teams e.g. test matches, international football/rugby matches and international athletics etc. to be available on all radio/television channels.

★ Discourage the multi-ownership of newspapers. Encourage responsible investigative journalism and media self-control.
Ensure that the Advertising Standards Authority, the Press Complaints Commission (which regulates printed newspapers and

magazines) and OFCOM (the UK's broadcasting watchdog) maintain and seek to improve standards of decency, truth and balance.

★ Discourage the portrayal of gratuitous screen violence and inappropriate sex scenes in all TV/films and impose a 'nine o' clock watershed' on all channels. Discourage parents and carers from allowing children to have a TV in their bedrooms where they can watch programmes unsupervised and seek to limit mobile phones, owned by children, access to the Internet. Uphold a statutory system of age ratings for video games.

Ensure the content of adverts and trailers for films screened in cinemas meets the same guidelines as the certificate rating of the film they are showing alongside.

★Although the internet is not a basic requirement for living, it is a useful tool. National access to broadband with improved download speeds would be useful and current plans should be continued as quickly as is practicably and commercially possible.

People should be encouraged to act within the law with regard to the illegal downloading of music and films, but Internet Service Providers also have a responsibility to take action against people who repeatedly infringe copyright by illegally sharing music and film files.

Art, Heritage And Sport

Creativity is part of the human personality and should be encouraged in every person, whatever their age or ability, in every genre.

Competitive sport and sport for pleasure are useful ways of maintaining a healthy lifestyle and socialising with others. First class sporting facilities should therefore be available to all who wish to use them.

The Olympic Games were originally intended to be a demonstration of sporting excellence. They have now become however, a show of entertaining extravagance. The aim of the Olympic Games therefore needs to be refocused on athletes simply giving of their best whether they win a medal or not, and also to act as a catalyst for encouraging people to engage in sport at every level both now and in the future.

★ Increase the budget of the Arts Council. Promote the expansion of the British Film industry.
★ Allow free access to all publicly owned cultural centres including art galleries and 'user friendly' museums and reduce the cost of participating in activities offered by sports centres.

> *'Increase the level of appreciation of, and participation in, arts, culture and leisure activities.'*
> (Alliance Party of Northern Ireland Election Manifesto 2005, p.24)

★ Enforce a restriction on all professional clubs in all sports to allow two players only born outside the UK to play in the first team. End business sponsorship of national teams.

Defence

For centuries, nations have learnt to make war. The C21st demands that we now learn how to make peace. The primary role of the armed forces, therefore, should be one of peacekeeping and rapid response in times of humanitarian crisis.

In order to fulfil those requirements, the armed forces should be highly trained, well equipped and thoughtfully deployed, thus avoiding the need to be 'wise after the event' when lives have already been lost. The decision to send service men and women into any conflict should take into consideration the reasons for engaging in that conflict, its likely outcome and the timescale required for rebuilding.

It is clear that since the Second World War, nuclear weapons have had no effect on deterring regional wars or international terrorism. There needs, therefore, to be a clear move away from the acquisition of nuclear arms both nationally and internationally and a pursuing of other means of national self-defence.

★ Review the current capacity of the armed forces in the light of possible future deployments whilst ensuring a high level of investment in training, technology and equipment. Ensure ample support for service personnel and their families and guarantee a sufficient level of compensation for those injured whilst engaged in their duties. Minimum age of entry into the armed forces 20 years.

> 'Those serving in our Armed Forces are vitally important to us, so we must take care of the people most important to them. A Conservative Government will support service families. They deserve decent homes, good schools for their children, and the chance to spend as much time as possible with their families.'
> (Conservative Party Election Manifesto 2005, p.25)

★   Maintain a UK 'rapid response unit' to assist those in need of famine relief or assistance following a natural disaster.

Encourage the development of an impartial, adequately resourced, professional and pro-active United Nations Rapid Reaction Force with a role to prevent conflict, enforce peace and assist in long-term development.

> 'The capacity of the United Nations for peace-keeping and conflict prevention should be strengthened.'
> (Plaid Cymru Election Manifesto 2005, p.15)

> 'Alliance priorities are to-
> Urge the UK Government to support the creation of a Standing Rapid Reaction Force for the United Nations.'
> (Alliance Party of Northern Ireland Election Manifesto 2005, p.26)

★   Discourage individual countries policing the world.

★   Pursue multilateral nuclear disarmament negotiations and ensure a phased decommissioning of Britain's Trident nuclear system. Honour existing contracts, but phase out arms sales to other countries. Seek an international agreement to control the sale of arms worldwide. Enable companies that manufacture armaments to diversify into areas of peaceful production.

Reduce research into nuclear, chemical and biological weapons, but increase research into anti-missile missiles and radar technology.

*   Maintain current involvement in N.A.T.O. whilst assisting in the review of its long-term role and purpose.

*   Clearly define in law what constitutes a 'matter of national security' and allow all other information to be available to public scrutiny.

Pollution and the Environment

Pollution in whatever form is not only unsightly but a product of the misuse of the world's resources. It is everyone's responsibility and waste needs to be reduced by not only adopting a zero waste policy, but a 100% recycling policy. One nation's pollution affects all nations and will, in time, assist in destroying the fragile balance of nature. We are therefore duty bound to co-operate with other countries and, where possible, give a lead in reducing pollution to a minimum.

No country has the right to abuse or monopolise the earth's resources as all nations have equal shares in the earth and, by the same token, are all stewards of its diverse riches. Currently, many of the earth's natural resources are being depleted faster than they can be replaced. The future therefore demands that we all live sustainable lifestyles and avoid wasteful consumption of natural assets. Thus, encouragement needs to be given to educating people at all levels of society of the true economic and environmental costs of their actions and to illustrate the potential savings from the efficient use of resources and the reduction of waste, whilst highlighting the potential for new markets in environmentally friendly products, services and expertise.

Developed countries need to act with determination to keep pollutants in the atmosphere as low as possible, through their own carbon emission reduction and by offering assistance to poorer countries, to help them develop low carbon alternatives.

The environment we all share not only has value in itself, but is also there to sustain human life. Its protection and continuing viability is therefore of paramount importance to the human race if our children's children are to enjoy its beauty and bounty.

'We only have one earth. Everything we produce and consume comes from this one finite resource. The central aim of green politics is to reduce

MAURICE JONES

our burden or 'ecological footprint' on the planet to a sustainable level. This means we have to protect our environment. Continued reliance on industrial and agricultural processes that use up natural resources and produce ever-increasing amounts of pollution and waste is unsustainable. It is also inequitable as, increasingly, the world's poorest countries bear the greatest burden from resource depletion and environmental destruction.'
(Green Party Election Manifesto 2005, p.20)

'A commitment to safeguarding our environment lies deep in Conservative thinking. We instinctively understand the importance of conservation, natural beauty and our duty of stewardship of the earth.'
(Conservative Election Manifesto 2005, p.22)

★ Establish a properly resourced waste management strategy based on waste reduction, the proper disposal of waste by industry and individuals and the expansion of re-use facilities in the UK. All packaging, i.e. for food/commercial, to be recyclable where possible.
    Discourage junk mail. Adopt zero tolerance to litter.
    End the incineration of waste.

'Our growing mountains of waste represent economic inefficiency - resources we have failed to re-use. Using systemic thinking across the entire lifecycle of products and services we can, like nature, recycle all our domestic and industrial waste.

As a first step we will ... legislate to reduce packaging, outlaw incineration, set standards for the recycled contents of products, and stabilise the market in recyclable materials.'
(Green Party Election Manifesto 2005, p.20)

'A properly resourced and effective Waste Management Strategy - based on waste reduction, re-use and re-cycling, at all levels in the waste production stream.

The rejection of incineration as a means of disposing of domestic, industrial or agricultural waste.'
(Sinn Fein Executive Summary 2005, p.5)

'The UK Independence Party is strongly in favour of measures - imposed and enforced by our own government and local authorities - that minimise the production of waste and maximise the amount that is recycled.'
(UK Independence Party Election Manifesto 2005, p.10)

★   Re-establish a controlling interest by government in the water industry by purchasing 51% of the shares.

Reduce water wastage through the replacement of faulty pipes.

All homes to be fitted as soon as possible with water meters, with the cost being shared equally between the customer and the government.

Encourage consumers to conserve water by operating a pay structure that has an initial flat rate, after which, the more you use the more you pay. Enhance the commercial/leisure use of inland waterways and canals.

Seek an international ban on the dumping of waste materials in the sea, particularly plastic waste.

★   Encourage the recovery and safe disposal of redundant appliances.

★   Government and local authorities to have binding targets for reducing their own carbon footprint. Closely monitor industrial emissions of pollutants and penalise those companies who do not seek their progressive reduction.

★ Work with other nations to globally reduce greenhouse gas emissions.

Agriculture, Fisheries and the Countryside

Governments have a responsibility to ensure the development of a coordinated rural policy that promotes the continuance of vibrant rural communities, managed tourism, home based businesses and a thriving agricultural sector.

Although there will always be a need for some food imports, the United Kingdom has the practical 'hands on' expertise and the science/technology to improve its food security by increasing food production in a sustainable way.

The quest in the past for cheap food has encouraged a misuse of animals, birds and farm land and created a tendency towards wastage of the food purchased. The emphasis therefore should be on encouraging farmers to produce high quality, realistically priced food, in an environmentally friendly way, that promotes the very best animal/bird welfare, reduces greenhouse gas emissions from the food system and limits chemical use, with guarantees from Central and Local Government to purchase food produced in the UK to supply, hospitals, prisons, schools etc. Also, to help people, particularly children, to reconnect with where their food comes from and how it is produced.

In order to reduce the amount of food thrown away, emphasis also needs to be given to promoting advice on good meal planning and shopping, wise portion sizes, effective fridge and freezer storage and how to create interesting recipes for using up leftovers.

For the countryside to be enjoyed by future generations, it needs to be protected from large scale development and coastal erosion via a long-term flood defence strategy. The countryside is more than open fields between towns and cities. As people we need to be released from the confines of our streets, released from the noise of our world. We need to be encouraged to stop and stare, to relax and enjoy local natural habitats.

We need space to find ourselves and we need peace to find God.

'Those involved in farming and fishing have had to cope with intense price pressures, imports and falling incomes. This had led thousands of workers to leave the industries, resulting in further decline to rural economies. This, in turn, increases our food and economic insecurity: we become more dependent on food supplies from overseas, with ever-longer supply chains controlled by transnational corporations. This reduces the revenue circulating in local economies and contributes to a vicious cycle that has to be broken.' (Green Party Election Manifesto 2005, p.22)

★ Bring an end to battery and other forms of intensive farming with the process of change commencing with immediate effect. Promote economic free-range and organic farming. Ban the growing of GM crops but encourage scientific research that assists in improving the natural production of food. Encourage the gradual reduction of chemicals used in farming. Promote research into maintaining a healthy honey bee population. Ban the live export of animals from the

UK and all imported fur products. Uphold the ban on the hunting of foxes with dogs.

> 'The SSP stands for: An end to battery farming and other forms of intensive farming.'
> (Scottish Socialist Party Election Manifesto 2005, p.34)
> 'Alliance opposes the introduction of genetically-modified crops.'
> (Alliance Party of Northern Ireland Election Manifesto 2005, p.21)

> 'Develop a strategy of organic food production. This will cover research, development, standards and marketing, and address all parts of the food chain. We will seek practical ways to promote the production of more locally produced organic food.'
> (Alliance Party of Northern Ireland Election Manifesto 2005, p.21)

> '... the Green Party would:
> End live animal exports from the UK
> Implement a full ban on the production and sale of eggs produced from hens kept in battery cages (including 'enriched' cages)
> Ban all imports of fur products'
> (Green Party Election Manifesto 2005, p.21)

> 'Ban the hunting of mammals with dogs.
> Hunting foxes and deer, as well as hare coursing, is incompatible with animal welfare.'
> (Alliance Party of Northern Ireland Election Manifesto 2005, p.18)

★ All supermarkets and food shops to only stock imported food produced to the same welfare and quality standards which apply to British farmers. (All retail outlets to only stock items e.g. clothing, that have been ethically produced and to promote Fairtrade products.)

Ensure one consistent standard system of food/drink labelling which clearly informs the customer of contents, nutritional values, country of origin and level of health risk. Ensure a wider range of food packaging to provide smaller portions for those who are single or elderly. Encourage the growth of courses that develop skills in home cooking, food planning and encourage people to eat more in-season fruit and vegetables. Direct supermarkets to substantially reduce 'food miles' by sourcing locally whenever possible. Local shopkeepers to be given priority by councils considering 'out of town' supermarket planning applications. Encourage the growth of farmer's markets.

> *'Britain's farmers operate to some of the highest animal welfare standards in the world and help to preserve the countryside for all of us to enjoy... We will support initiatives, such as farmers' markets and local food projects, that enable British customers to support Britain's farmers.'*
> (Conservative Party Election Manifesto 2005, p.23)

> *'Extend compulsory country of origin labelling. We endorse the efforts of the Food Standards Agency to improve food labelling policy.'*
> (Alliance Party of Northern Ireland Election Manifesto 2005, p.21)

★ Encourage small farmers to form co-operatives and to consider complimentary diversification. Maintain the tenanted farm sector.

> *'Protect farmers from the excessive buying powers of big business by allowing the expansion of farmers' co-operatives.'*
> (UK Independence Party Election Manifesto 2005, p.8)

★ Withdraw from the Common Agricultural Policy. Encourage the reopening of local abattoirs.

> *'Leaving the CAP will ... remove a vast amount of unnecessary bureaucracy that is such a severe burden on small farmers... sensible revision of ineffective health regulations will allow the reopening of small local abattoirs, removing a major cause of long distance transport of live animals. This will also prevent the spread of disease and promote another of UKIP's aims - the marketing of locally produced food.'*
> (UK Independence Party Election Manifesto 2005, p.8)

★ Promote countryside conservation and support the Linking Environment and Farming (LEAF) initiative. Promote landscape and wildlife conservation in urban and city areas. Encourage the planting of broad-leaved trees/woodland management and an increase in the general planting of woodland by promoting biomass wood boiler home/commercial heating systems fuelled by wood chip and wood pellets.

Encourage the planting of trees on landfill sites.

★ Encourage councils to work closely with farmers and landowners to ensure that infill parcels of land and, in villages, agricultural land adjacent to the village envelope, is used for the expansion of self-funding allotments. Encourage the nationwide development of the 'landshare' scheme that links people who want to grow their own food with those who have spare land/garden space available.

★ End the growing of food crops specifically for bio-fuels. Encourage research into the use of the waste from food crops (e.g. stalks and leaves), the production of bio-fuels from non-food materials (e.g. rice-straw, wheat-straw, waste products from the forestry industry and lignin – a carbon-rich material produced as a waste product of paper production) and the production of genuinely sustainable bio-fuels such as algae. Also, encourage research into a) Anaerobic digestion, which converts organic matter such as food waste or pig slurry, into biogas and fertiliser and b) In-vessel composting which turns food and garden waste into compost.

★ Increase the level of investment in sea defences around the United Kingdom whilst monitoring sea level rise so as to ensure adequate protection and contingencies in the years to come, without flooding areas of land. Increase the level of investment in flood protection from rivers and surface water and initiate a creative nationwide response to resolving drainage problems. Discourage dredging in the North Sea.

★ Withdraw from the European Union Common Fisheries Policy and instead pursue an agreed long-term strategy for management/conservation of UK fish stocks, rebuild the fisheries protection fleet, stipulate mesh sizes of nets and set up temporary 'fallow' zones to allow stocks to recover.

> 'The UK Independence Party will ... put in place an agreed long-term strategy for management and conservation.
>
> Re-establish British control over our coastal waters with sufficient rebuilding of our fisheries protection fleet to enforce this. Fishing licences to stipulate acceptable practices such as mesh sizes of nets.

MAURICE JONES

Fishing prohibited in temporary 'fallow' zones to allow stocks to recover.'
(UK Independence Party Election Manifesto 2005, p.8)

End intensive fish farming and oppose destructive fishing practices in other parts of the world. Fully implement and seek to extend the Marine and Coastal Access Act.

Northern Ireland

The problems associated with Northern Ireland are not insoluble and much progress has been made in recent years. Encouragement therefore needs to be given to people at all levels of society to further the peace process by promoting continuous dialogue, fostering open minds and trust between neighbours, integrating education, increasing funding for local community relations projects and helping those whose raison d'etre has been the furtherance of paramilitary activity or sectarianism to understand their time has now been and gone, forever.

Although geographically separate, Northern Ireland is very much an integral part of the United Kingdom and should always remain so.

★ Maintain the constitutional position of Northern Ireland within the United Kingdom. Promote integration in every sphere of life based on the principal of mutual respect. Increase funding for community-based projects that promote 'good relations', in particular, locally based arts and cultural projects.

'The Progressive Unionist Party is fully committed to maintaining and strengthening the present constitutional position of Northern Ireland within the United Kingdom. The Party shall work by all democratic means to ensure that there will be no change to the United Kingdom or Northern Ireland's place within it.

The Party is fully committed to the development of a new era of peace and stability in Northern Ireland. This peace should be based on the principal of mutual respect.

The Progressive Unionist Party is committed to working for the reconstruction of our society. To achieve this goal we advocate participative community action. We encourage our members to work at local level for the development of community education and training programmes, which discover, draw out and develop the strengths and potential of the whole community. We will campaign for increased levels of core funding for community-based projects that enable capacity building and the promotion of 'good relations'.

The Progressive Unionist Party believes that community development must go hand in hand with cultural expression. We believe that community based arts projects can strengthen the confidence of a neighbourhood. Thus we support increased funding for locally based arts and cultural projects.

In Northern Ireland as a whole we believe that support for the arts can provide a dynamic for increased respect and understanding. Thus we support the development of single and multi identity projects.'
(Progressive Unionist Party Election Manifesto 2005, p.3-4)

'We are committed to building a united community, and creating a shared future where people can live and learn, work and play together in safety.

However, building good relations in this society cannot just be a matter for government, it is a responsibility for civil society and indeed every person in society.'
(Alliance Party of Northern Ireland Election Manifesto 2005, p.7)

Foreign Policy and Overseas Aid

Although it may be tempting to condemn other nations for acting in ways we consider inhumane or unjust, it is important to ensure that, with regard to foreign policy, the United Kingdom does not itself act hypocritically and that, as a nation, we earn the right to have our voice heard at an international level.

Every nation is entitled to defend itself, but should expect an international response if it is slaughtering its own citizens or acting aggressively towards innocent civilians in another nation. Having said that, no nation has the right to invade another unilaterally; even in response to a terrorist threat.

All nations, though, have a responsibility to engage warring parties in high level diplomacy and offer security to innocent civilians via well-equipped, well-armed, pro-active United Nations peace enforcers. We have only partially discerned how to deal with the threat of terrorism. Essentially terrorism is a state of mind, based on a set of values and beliefs. Engaging in a 'War on Terror' with C21st weaponry and C20 tactics can be costly both in financial and humanitarian terms and counter-productive. Single nation 'liberating' forces are easy targets for militants and often outstay their welcome, making them a part of the problem not a part of the solution. As long drawn-out guerrilla warfare tends to favour the 'weaker' side, to effectively combat terrorism the underlying reasons for the terrorists state of mind need to be understood and challenged and the hearts and minds of the oppressed nation won over, before any lives are sacrificed through military intervention.

The invasion of Iraq was unwisely pre-emptive. As it was born out of a false pretext, insufficient time was given for high level diplomacy and those invading acted unilaterally. Also, little consideration was given to rebuilding Iraq after the invasion. Although those servicemen and women who served in Iraq deserve the highest commendation, those who made the decision to go to war, now need to fully justify their actions.

Cement walls create barriers and barriers prevent reconciliation, which usually brings suffering to those on both sides of the divide and allows dissidents opportunity to sow seeds of distrust. Nations whose indigenous population can learn to live at peace and forgive, forget and put aside their suspicions, are nations who will not only progress and prosper, but will show the rest of the world how to live.

Every nation has a responsibility to assist those in other nations who are oppressed by poverty or injustice not because they deserve our aid, but because they are human beings.

They are people with names, hopes and fears. They are people who desire their dignity to be restored not with continuous 'handouts', but by practical compassion, so they can progress from living on 'charity' and take responsibility for their own welfare. It is simply unacceptable that, in the C21st, millions of people around the world do not enjoy even the basic necessities of life. We need to change our thinking. Those who would be considered 'poor' in the Western World are affluent, or often opulent, when compared with those living in underdeveloped nations. At best, charitable giving through 'Band Aid' or 'Comic Relief' or other organisations or charitable events, although helpful, can only have a limited effect. Thus comprehensive, long–term solutions are now required to overcome problems that have been allowed to deteriorate for generations, so that all nations can become self-supporting.

> *'Our priorities are to ensure that richer countries become responsible stewards of creation, share the resources and wealth of our planet and protect the environment in every way that they can. We will promote the global common good through respect for the rule of law and by strengthening international organisations such as the UN. We will pursue policies that challenge the root causes of injustice, such as wars, generalised violence, persecution, human rights abuses, the arms trade, the crippling debt burden and unfair trade practices that distort the economies of poor countries.'*
>
> (Christian Peoples Alliance Election Manifesto 2005, p. Britain Loving Its Neighbours)

★   Maintain diplomatic contact with, but closely monitor and challenge countries that operate oppressive racial or human rights policies, restrict religious freedom and/or obstruct the education and empowerment of women. Encourage stable, humane governance in all nations.

★   Operate strict controls to ensure that aid directly assists those in need, rather than benefits corrupt governments or officials. Focus aid on the least developed countries and on providing the basics of living e.g. food, clean water, sanitation, health services, education and employment.

As far as is possible work with the leaders of all nations and encourage countries in areas of conflict to take responsibility for ending corruption and insurgency.

> *'Aid given to poorer countries often gets into the wrong hands. Yet projects to help communities in the third world to help themselves lack finance and rely on charitable aid.*

What will we do?

Give effective aid directly where it is needed, diverting overseas aid from going into the pockets of corrupt third world leaders.'

(Veritas Election Manifesto 2005, Overseas Aid)

★   Increase the Overseas Aid and Development budget to 5% of gross national income.

★   Seek to establish a permanent United Nations contingency fund for emergencies and famine relief. Review with other nations the effectiveness of the International Monetary Fund regarding its role in assisting developing countries. Actively promote the progression of the United Nations' Millennium Development Goals, which include reducing child mortality rates, fighting diseases such as AIDS, ending poverty and improving global partnerships to promote development.

★   Encourage intermediate technology and small-scale farming in underdeveloped countries.

★   Encourage fair free trade and the reduction of protectionism by rich countries by seeking to change international trade laws via the World Trade Organisation and ending export subsidies.

'International trade laws which favour rich countries by robbing the world's poorest people will be tackled by a change in WTO rules. Export subsidies that damage the livelihoods of poor communities around the world will be ended. A rise in trade will generate many times more resources than given through aid or debt relief.'

(Christian Peoples Alliance Election Manifesto 2005, p. Britain Loving Its Neighbours)

★   Request that states who receive aid respect the fundamental human rights of their people. Seek to rewrite international trade laws so as to favour poor nations.

★   Seek to restrict multinational companies from profiting at the expense of people and the environment and support international moves to ensure multinational companies declare the profits they make in each country within which they operate, so that poor countries are able to collect the tax revenue which is rightfully theirs. Pursue the cancellation of the world's poorest countries' unpayable debts.

> 'Multinational companies will be held to account for the way they do business, especially their treatment of the environment.'
> (Christian Peoples Alliance Election Manifesto 2005, p. Britain Loving Its Neighbours)

★   Seek an end to conditional debt cancellation – such as inviting in foreign corporations and privatising services. Assist underdeveloped countries to restructure their economies along sustainable lines.

> 'We will press for reforms in trade, aid and debt and so release resources for developing countries to tackle vital issues such as HIV/AIDS and lack of access to safe water, sanitation, healthcare and education. Aid will be given in grants and not loans and not tied to poor countries opening up their markets or inviting in powerful multinationals from rich countries. We want the unpayable debts of the world's poorest countries to be cancelled in full without strings attached.'
> (Christian Peoples Alliance Election Manifesto 2005, p. Britain Loving its Neighbours)

> 'Call for 100% cancellation of debt from the most highly indebted countries, as burdensome debt repayments prevent scarce resources being invested into development.'
> (Alliance Party of Northern Ireland Election Manifesto 2005, p.26)

> '… debt destabilises national economies because the need to service the debt overrides any potential long-term vision for the future. Destabilised countries that feel they have no alternatives are more likely to go to war or be involved in terrorism. As well as being a matter of social justice, it is therefore also in our national security interest to reduce the debt of the poorest countries in order to help them become more stable.'
> (Green Party Election Manifesto 2005, p.29)

'Support the Make Poverty History campaign to address developing world debt, for higher aid, and fairer trade.'
(Alliance Party of Northern Ireland Election Manifesto 2005, p.26)

★   Honour those who lost their lives in the Iraq war, but consider legal action against politicians responsible for the invasion.

'There were no weapons of mass destruction, there was no serious and current threat, and inspectors were denied the time they needed to finish their job … Britain must never again support an illegal military intervention.'
(Liberal Democrat Election Manifesto 2005, p.14-15)

'A Green government would not have gone to war in Iraq. Such an act was against international law and lacked the support of the UN. It was a profoundly misjudged act of foreign policy which has killed thousands, reduced Iraq to chaos, and left the UK dangerously exposed to global terrorism …'
(Green Party Election Manifesto 2005, p.28)

'The Christian Peoples Alliance opposed the government's pre-emptive and illegal war against Iraq as a breach of Chapter 7 of the UN Charter. We warned it would lead to innumerable civilian casualties and make the West more vulnerable to terrorist attack.'
(Christian Peoples Alliance Election Manifesto 2005, p. Britain Loving Its Neighbours)

★   Seek to understand and overcome the root causes of terrorism.

'Although of course there is a need to protect ourselves against possible terrorist attacks, it is important also to strike at the roots of terrorism. These are often about the injustices suffered by the poor of the world. Unless basic injustices are tackled in a serious way, there will be a further build-up in tension, terrorism, and conflict. Polices for justice are therefore policies for peace.'
(Plaid Cymru Election Manifesto 2005, p.15)

'A pro-active foreign and trade policy that addresses the root causes of

discontent in the poverty and injustice of the developing world is the best long-term strategy to tackle the threat of terrorism. Britain and its allies in the EU and US would do better to invest in schooling, a free media and environmental protection than bombing campaigns, spyware and ID cards. As Christian Democrats we would demonstrate an understanding of diverse religious motivations and acknowledge the alienation in the developing world caused by the materialism and individualism of western society.'
(Christian Peoples Alliance Election Manifesto 2005, p. Britain Loving Its Neighbours)

★ Initiate a phased withdrawal from Afghanistan, replacing British troops with United Nations peace enforcers. Assist the population of Afghanistan to rebuild their lives and their country and maintain their own security, but with the proviso that the Government upholds basic human rights, particularly with regard to women. Increase and strengthen diplomatic engagement with the leaders of Afghanistan, Pakistan and other surrounding countries.

★ Work for peace and reconciliation in the Middle East whilst supporting the right of Israel to exist as an independent, democratic, Jewish State with Jerusalem as its capital.
Seek the incorporation of the West Bank and Gaza Strip into Israel with Jews and Palestinians living side by side but free to hold their own individual religious beliefs or, assist those Palestinians who wish, to relocate to one of Israel's neighbours. Seek to maintain constructive dialogue with all parties.

'We will work for peace and reconciliation in the Middle East. This will not abrogate a responsibility to expose and alter Islamist threats to the integrity and security of the State of Israel.'
(Christian Peoples Alliance Election Manifesto 2005, p. Britain Loving Its Neighbours)

★ Reject torture in all its forms and in all circumstances.

★ Encourage and strengthen commonwealth links.

Europe

The European Coal and Steel Community was established after the Second World War as the first step towards averting a third European conflict. This underlying fear and consequent insecurity has spawned a Union based on the need to control via a central authority, a Union with aspirations to become an empire.

> *'What we have is the first non-imperial empire. We have 27 countries that fully decided to work together and pool their sovereignty. I believe this is a great construction and we should be proud of it.'*
> (Jose Barroso, President of the European Commission)

However, the further away the centre of government is from those for whom it legislates, the more insensitive and uniform that legislation becomes and the harder it is for those on the receiving end to 'own' that legislation and hold the legislators to account. It is important for the people of Europe to work together, but enforced unity only breeds disunity.

★ Formally withdraw from the European Union by repealing the 1972 European Communities Act and replace it with a free trade agreement. Encourage cooperation across Europe with regard to areas of common concern and mutual benefit e.g. the environment, investigating terrorist acts and criminal activity.

> *'Formal withdrawal from the EU will be achieved by repealing the 1972 European Communities Act. This will release us from obligations under EU treaties and re-establish the precedence of UK law over EU law. We shall immediately stop paying into the EU budget and we shall resume full independent participation in international bodies such as the World Trade Organisation. It will be possible to scrap some EU rules ... without delay. However, many other changes following independence will take more time. We would aim for a transition period of 2 years with the work managed by a cabinet committee, assisted by interested parties from all relevant sectors of the economy. One of its main tasks will be to govern the repeal or amendment of the mass of UK laws and statutory instruments that have originated in the EU, replacing them if necessary with laws that are in British interests alone. Other responsibilities of the transition*

committee will include the replacement of all the EU's 'common' policies including farming and fishing, with our own arrangements.'
(UK Independence Party Election Manifesto 2005, p.1)

'Few of the positive things we want to achieve can be done within the European Union. In fact, the EU project for political union is destroying what Europe could be - a continent of free, progressive, dynamic, self-governing nations.

Withdraw from the EU's failed institutions and repeal the European Communities Act 1972. If we are to be a world embracing nation- rather than 'little Europeans' it is time to recover our national self-government, our initiative and our enterprise.'
(The New Party Election Manifesto 2005, European Union)

'The EU is removing our ability to govern ourselves and make our own decisions about our future...

What will we do?

govern ourselves with our own Parliament in Westminster,
replace the Treaties on European Union with a free trade agreement.'
(Veritas Election Manifesto 2005, The European Union)

★   As there are currently two systems of measurement in the UK both used to varying degrees, allow the Imperial system and metric to run side by side.

Pets and Animal Welfare

All animals and birds, whether wild or tame, have a right to be treated with care. Their management both inside and outside of their natural habitat, therefore, needs to be carefully monitored.

★   Enhance and expand the work of the RSPCA and RSPB particularly in regard to the prosecution of those owners who fail to provide adequate care and attention for their pets, animals and birds.

Encourage a high standard of care for all animals kept in zoos. Develop the role of zoos in education and research and the reintroduction of captive bred stock into the wild. Closely monitor the welfare of animals in sport.

Encourage a high standard of care for all caged birds and animals. Tighten controls on the import of wild birds and animals.

'We will...guarantee high standards of animal welfare across the board for farm livestock, working animals and domestic pets ...'
(Liberal Democrat Election Manifesto 2005, p.16–17)

★ Maintain rabies prevention safeguards.

★ Ensure no animals are used in the testing of cosmetics, household products and for military purposes and end any unnecessary animal testing in medical research, whilst promoting research into non-animal alternatives.

'The SSP stands for: A ban on the testing of animals for cosmetics, household products and military purposes; and an end to unnecessary testing in medical research.'
(Scottish Socialist Party Election Manifesto 2005, p.34)

Home and Community

Gambling

There is no such thing as 'responsible' gambling. Gambling by its very nature is irresponsible and can become as addictive as any drug, resulting in serious financial consequences.

★ Ban the use of fixed-odds betting terminals. Increase the levy on off-course bookmakers. Ban all sponsorship and advertising by companies engaged in gambling. Restrict the number and limit the size of gambling outlets/casinos in a neighbourhood. Minimum gambling age 22 years. Ban advertisements for online gambling. Provide adequate counselling for those addicted to gambling. Repeal all legislation relating to the National Lottery. Encourage people to find adventure and meaning in their lives through means other than gambling.

'Are people really trying to get rich quick? Is that the motivation behind all this gambling? Certainly, the growth of the gambling culture is yet one more component of a 'more-more' society that fosters discontent with what we have.

But beyond the lure of sudden wealth, or even marginally increased resources, what the bet adds is risk, or perhaps more tellingly, adventure. People are looking for some adventure, for something that matters. And where else are they to find it? Most people don't find much meaning in their work. Our armed forces may be fighting ... but we are not engaged in the kind of war that galvanises the entire population behind some shared high and noble cause. So where is the adventure in life? Where is the risk? Where is the task that stretches us, the cause that invigorates us? Where is the activity that calls on our courage, that tests our mettle? Is not life in 21st century Britain somewhat trivial? But a bet puts me on edge, sets my sails to the wind. I could lose. I could win. But either way I have entered the fray. Better to have bet and lost than never to have bet at all.' (Mark Greene.)

Pornography

Pornography, portrayed in whatever way, exploits and dehumanises sex so that human beings are viewed as things and women in particular, as sex objects, rather than real people. Assistance therefore needs to be offered to those who find difficulty in achieving sexual fulfilment through relationship and a culture promoted that encourages respect for the human body and the person inside it. For those who wish to use sexual allurement for financial gain, help needs to be offered to them to find less ostentatious ways of achieving their ambition.

Although women may choose to sell themselves for sex, often there are other underlying reasons for their prostitution. Assistance therefore needs to be given to protecting prostitutes from being exploited through vulnerability, coercion or threats by offering them help into other forms of employment, offering drug therapy and in order to deter clients, ensuring that those who pay for sex are always charged with committing a criminal offence.

★ Strengthen the law relating to the sale and production of hard and soft pornography and its portrayal on the Internet. Encourage newsagents not to stock pornographic newspapers. As top-shelf stocking doesn't stop children observing pornographic magazines, and shops are not consistent in heights of material displayed, ensure under 18s are not able to view or purchase them.

★ Increase sentences for those who solicit prostitutes or promote prostitution. Increase assistance to prostitutes to enable them to change their lifestyle. Substantially raise the licence charge for lap-dancing clubs, sex shops and sex cinemas and enable Unitary District Councils to control their spread.

Encourage the police to regularly inspect brothels, investigate claims of sexual exploitation and prosecute those who advertise people for sex.

Citizens Advice Bureaux

★ Encourage the expansion of independent advice centres and the development of 'one stop' Citizens Advice Bureaux throughout the United Kingdom.

'Ensure adequate funding for Citizens Advice Bureaux and other independent advice centres. This is essential to help people disadvantaged by inadequate advice on social security, debt, housing and employment.'
(Alliance Party of Northern Ireland Election Manifesto 2005, p.22)

Organisations for Young People

★ Encourage the development of uniformed organisations for children/teenagers, the expansion of the Duke of Edinburgh's Scheme and voluntary work. Encourage a wider variety of youth facilities in every community that enable young people to develop a healthy attitude to leisure in an environment that raises self-esteem and respect for others.

'The SSP stands for: Funding of local youth facilities in every community run democratically by and for young people.'
(Scottish Socialist Party Election Manifesto 2005, p.37)

Libraries

★   Develop and expand the range of services offered by libraries. All libraries to offer on Saturday afternoons, free activities for children and parents such as the MAD (Me and Dad) scheme in Suffolk

> *' We should ensure that the valuable role of libraries in the community is protected.'*
> (Ulster Democratic Unionist Party Election Manifesto 2005, p.25)

> *'Enhance the Library Service. We would adequately resource and publicise initiatives such as mobile libraries, which will particularly benefit older people and those living in rural areas.'*
> (Alliance Party of Northern Ireland Election Manifesto 2005, p.24)

Marriage

A marriage between a man and a woman based on a loving, lifelong relationship offers the best foundation for a stable society and a secure home environment and gives balanced role models for children. All other forms of partnerships therefore need to be considered in that light.

★   Minimum age of consent for marriage 20 years. Repeal the Civil Partnership Act which enables same-sex couples to obtain legal recognition of their relationship. Vigorously oppose polygamy by ensuring all 'religious' marriages are registered.

> *'Children brought up and nurtured within the stability and commitment of marriage are significantly more likely to be socially adjusted and educationally successful than those of any other arrangements. Children*

living with co-habiting couples for instance are 50% more likely to have mental health problems than those with married couples. ... there is a direct correlation between the decline of marriage in Britain and the rise in adolescent anti-social behaviour, the yob culture and teenage pregnancies.'
(Christian Peoples Alliance Election Manifesto 2005, p.3)

★ Fully support the Forced Marriage Act which prohibits an individual from being married against their will.

The Post Office

Post offices are a vital element in sustaining and improving community life both in villages and the city. They are more than just a place to do business, they act as a meeting point, a place to relate, a place to gently monitor the well-being of others.

★ Reopen post offices where viable, particularly in rural areas, possibly locating them in pubs or village shops.

★ Royal Mail to have a monopoly on letter delivery and to continue with phased modernisation in order to maintain efficient same-price letter deliveries across the United Kingdom for six days a week.

★ Promote the development of a Post Bank in order to offer a higher level of financial/banking services throughout all post offices. Distribution of benefits and pensions through the Post Office Card Account to remain on a permanent basis. Maintain the option of purchasing television licences and paying all other bills, over-the-counter in all post offices.

'Our priority is to secure a viable future for the post office network, by developing a business plan based on providing a combination of commercial services, benefits transactions and government information. This will help keep more post offices open. We will maintain the obligation on Royal Mail to provide universal same-price delivery of letters throughout the UK.'
(Liberal Democrat Election Manifesto 2005, p.12-13)

Royal Mail to be part owned by the Government and part owned by employee shareholders.

New Years Honours List

New Years Honours List to award those who have shown an outstanding level of dedication and sacrifice outside of their paid work, particularly in their home and /or community. Awards to be based on nominations received from the general public.

British Heritage

Churches and secular buildings that are of historic importance/interest and a recognised part of British heritage to be protected and supported by state funding.

CHAPTER FOUR

Healing the Nation

'Then the land had rest from war.'

Joshua 14:15

How do you heal a nation? Where do you start? What needs to change? The system? Everyone else? All those nebulous things we blame for making our life difficult? Or is the real answer closer to home. Something more personal. To heal this nation is it you who needs to change? Or me? Or both of us?

Many of my generation, the post Second World War generation, have lived privileged lives. Whereas those who endured the war suffered the scourge of deprivation, those of my generation, who have been fortunate enough to live in the Western world, have suffered from the scourge of excess. We have enjoyed untold advances in healthcare, untold disposable income, untold leisure facilities and an untold supply of food. Modern technology has given us access to all the earth's bounty at reduced cost. With this eye-catching, mouth-watering abundance available at the click of a button, our guiding principle has become, 'all human beings were 'born to shop'.

In their book *Jubilee Manifesto* Michael Schluter and John Ashcroft comment,

'Consumerism and economic growth seem to provide not just something to work for, but something to live for.'

However, there is no such thing as a free meal.

Our yearning to 'have it all' and more besides has not only had a negative effect on our relationships with each other but also on the earth's finite resources. Unless, therefore, we change our way of living now and seek to live balanced lives, our children's children are set to inherit a nation and a world that is substantially impoverished in both those areas.

But can Christians and others, desiring to see a healed, truly united, United Kingdom, with the changes to national life that would bring, really make a difference? Schluter and Ashcroft continue,

> 'Some will reject the idea of any biblically-based concept of bringing about global change as utopian, and point to texts suggesting the growing power and influence of evil leading up to the return of Christ. However, in the parable of the wheat and the weeds, Jesus tells his disciples that both the kingdom and its enemies will grow until the end of the age (Matt. 13:36-43); and it seems also from the parable that both what causes good to flourish and what 'causes sin' will also continue to grow until the end comes (Matt. 13:41).'

Thus they make clear, that not only is change possible, but that for the Christian it is more than a 'fanciful notion', a 'good idea', something to be considered at a later date. Seeking to heal this nation is an obligation. For Christ's disciples wherever they live, young or old, rich or poor, woman or man there is nowhere to turn, nowhere to hide, no excuse that can gain God's approval. His heart is for His disciples to act and to act now.

Schluter and Ashcroft conclude,

> 'The biblical approach to bringing about social change is not by violent revolution, nor by training a small political elite, but by every disciple of Christ 'practising and teaching [communicating] the law' (Matt. 5:19), which is summarized by the commandments to love God and love neighbour (Matt. 22:37-40). For all of us who are Christ's disciples, the imperative is to transform society ...
>
> We are given the mandate, the incentive and the agenda. It is time to act.'

It is easy to shut the front door on a nation that has lost its way, to draw the curtains, pour ourselves a drink, settle back on the sofa, switch on the TV or computer and loose ourselves in a fantasy world that entertains and anesthetises us. Do I have a responsibility of care towards my neighbour? Yes? No? Maybe? Or is compassion the responsibility of others? For Christians, there is no choice. Jesus Christ was a servant King. He demonstrated how His followers should live. His call to Christians in the United Kingdom and indeed across the world is to turn away from selfish living and to serve in whatever way they can their neighbour, those they know in the community and those they have never even met. Those who live on the other side of their front door.

Those who live on the other side of our comfort zone.

'The whole Christian thing is not just about going up to heaven after we die, but it is about bringing God's Kingdom to earth. THIS IS THE GOSPEL THAT SHOULD COMFORT THE DISTURBED AND DISTURB THE COMFORTABLE. And that means REVOLUTION. It is a revolution that sets both the oppressed and the oppressors free, a revolution that dances and laughs...a revolution that aches with the world. It is a revolution not just for saints and prophets and celebrities, but a revolution of ordinary radicals who live in ways that do not conform to the patterns of this world...'
Shane Claiborne

NOTES

Introduction

Adapted from the *Emperor's New Clothes*, Hans Christian Andersen

Chapter One

Maurice Jones, *Goodbye Great Britain*.
Sue Palmer, *Toxic Childhood*, Orion Books Ltd, 2007, p.34
The R Factor, Michael Schluter and David Lee, Hodder and Stoughton Ltd, 1993, p.157-158.
Votewise, Nick Spencer, SPCK, 2004, p.15
Polly Toynbee, *guardian,* Tuesday 17 March 2009

Chapter Two
New International Version, *Disciple's Study Bible*, Holman Bible Publishers, 1988, p.564
Elaine Storkey, *Word on the Street*, The Old Hall Press, 2003, p. 27-29
Roy McCloughry, *The Eye of the Needle*, Inter-Varsity Press, 1990, p.55
David Derbyshire, *Daily Telegraph*, 21 September 2004, cited in R briefing, The Relationships Foundation, Issue 48: March
    Robert Kennedy, 1968, cited in *The Triple Test*, Relationships Foundation, 2009, p.9
Richard Donkin, *Financial Times*, 14 October 2004, cited in R briefing, The Relationships Foundation, Issue 48: March

Chapter Three
The Holy Bible, Living Bible Edition, Kingsway Publications, 1994, p.603

Green Party Election Manifesto 2005

Scottish Socialist Party Election Manifesto 2005

Veritas Election Manifesto 2005

The R Option, Michael Schluter and David John Lee, The Relationships Foundation, 2003, p.51

Liberal Democrat Election Manifesto 2005

Plaid Cymru Election Manifesto 2005

Conservative Election Manifesto 2005

Alliance Party of Northern Ireland Election Manifesto 2005

Keith Tondeur, *Your Money and Your Life*, SPCK, 2003, p. 87

ProLife Election Manifesto 2005

The New Party Election Manifesto 2005

Christian Peoples Alliance Election Manifesto 2005

Scottish Socialist Party Election Manifesto 2005

Sinn Fein Executive Summary 2005

Ulster Democratic Unionist Party Election Manifesto 2005

Janice Turner, *The Times*, Saturday March 28 2009, p.19

UK Independence Party Election Manifesto 2005

Melanie Phillips, *Daily Mail*, Thursday May 19th 2005 p.17

Progressive Unionist Party Election Manifesto 2005

Marie Fatayi-Williams, *For the Love of Anthony*, Hodder and Stoughton, 2007, p. x

Jose Barroso, *Daily Telegraph*, 18/7/07, cited in Light for The Last Days, Autumn 2007, p.11

Mark Greene, *Christianity,* June 2006, p.52

Chapter Four

New International Version, *Disciple's Study Bible*, Holman Bible Publishers 1988, p.274

Jubilee Manifesto, edited by Michael Schluter and John Ashcroft, Inter-Varsity Press, 2005, p.327-330

Shane Claiborne, *Kingdom of Comfort*, Delirious?, Furious? Records, 2008

Special thanks to Alex Roxburgh whose comments and corrections have been invaluable.

ACKNOWLEDGEMENTS

Toxic Childhood by Sue Palmer (2007) Orion Books; reprinted with permission from the publisher.

For the Love of Anthony by Marie Fatayi-Williams (2007) Hodder and Stoughton; reprinted with permission.

The R Factor by Michael Schluter and David Lee (1993) Hodder and Stoughton; reprinted with permission.

Votewise by Nick Spencer (2004) SPCK.

'Bring in proportional representation' by Polly Toynbee, *The Guardian* 17 March 2009; reprinted with permission from Copyright Guardian News & Media Ltd 2009.

Word on the Street by Elaine Storkey (2003) The Old Hall Press; reprinted with permission from the author.

The Eye of the Needle by Roy McCloughry (1990) Inter-Varsity Press.

Jubilee Manifesto edited by Michael Schluter and John Ashcroft (2005) Inter-Varsity Press.

'Happiness is a WI, choir and charities' by David Derbyshire *Daily Telegraph*, 21 September 2004 c Telegraph Media Group Limited 2004; reprinted with permission.

Robert Kennedy, remarks made at the University of Kansas, March 18, 1968.

'Engaging employees in a happy relationship' by Richard Donkin, *Financial Times*, 14 October 2004; reprinted with kind permission of *Financial Times*.

The R Option by Michael Schluter and David John Lee (2003) The Relationships Foundation; reprinted with permission.

Your money or your life by Keith Tondeur (1996) SPCK by permission of SPCK.

'Listen girls: you'll never regret not doing it' by Janice Turner, *The*

Times, Saturday 28 March 2009 c *The Times* 28 March 2009; reprinted with permission from NI Syndication.

'Respect in the age of degradation' by Melanie Phillips *Daily Mail* 19 May 2005; reprinted with permission from Solo Syndication.

'Are people really trying to get rich quick?' by Mark Greene, *Christianity Magazine* June 2006, p.52 www.christianitymagazine.co.uk.

Kingdom of Comfort, Shane Claiborne, Delirious?, Furious? Records, 2008

Every effort has been made to contact all copyright holders. We apologise for any omissions, which will be corrected in any future edition.

MAURICE JONES